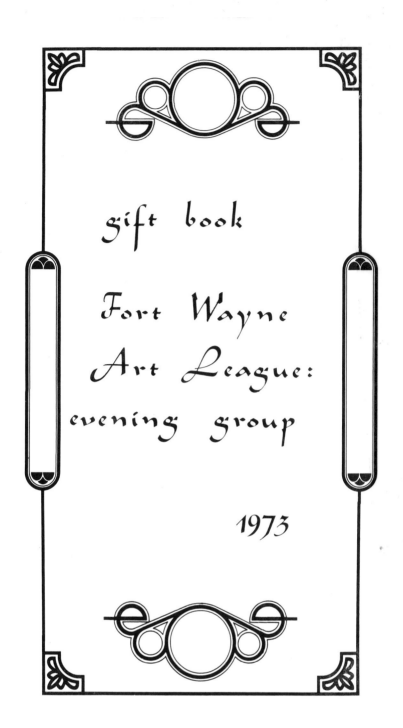

gift book

Fort Wayne

Art League:

evening group

1973

AJANTA

Plate 1

MADANJEET SINGH

AJANTA

Ajanta painting of the sacred and the secular

EDITA LAUSANNE

Copyright © 1965 by Madanjeet Singh/Edita S.A. Lausanne

Printed in Switzerland

CONTENTS

alankriyante kusumair mahīruhas
taḍidgaṇais toyavilambino ghanāhı
sarāṁsi mattabhramaraiḥ saroruhair
guṇair viśeṣādhigatais tu dehinaḥ ॥

" Blossoms are the ornaments of trees, it is flashes
of lightning that adorn the big rain clouds, the
lakes are adorned by lotuses and waterlilies with
their intoxicated bees: but virtues brought to perfection are the proper ornaments of living beings."

An Ajanta inscription.

Dedicated to the memory
of
Jawaharlal Nehru
(1889—1964)

I am deeply indebted to B. Ch. Chhabra, Joint Director General of Archaeology in India, for his cooperation generally and for his valuable advice especially in the transcription of the Pali and Sanskrit terms; and to Dhyanawati Singh for re-writing the summaries of the expansive *Jatakas* included in this book. My grateful thanks are also due to Michael Edwardes, W. G. Archer, Pheroza A. Wadia, Homi J. Bhabha, P. A. Marielwala, Mulk Raj Anand, G. C. Haloi, L. Roussel and other friends and colleagues without whose valuable criticisms and ungrudging help the compilation of this volume might not have been possible.

I wish to place on record my appreciation as well of the courtesy extended by the Government of India Archaeological Departments by giving me special facilities for working in the caves, and for the permission to reproduce some of the beautiful outlines of Ajanta painting by Sayed Ahmed.   *Madanjeet Singh.*

Plate 2

PREFACE

In the early nineteenth century, a few soldiers out hunting in the wild mountainous terrain near Ajanta were led by a cowherd to see some "tiger lairs." Thus, in the tradition of fairy-tales, these forbidding, almost inaccessible grottos were discovered to be rich treasure caverns of the oldest Buddhist art in the world. In 1822, three years after the discovery, William Erskine, in a paper read to the Bombay Literary Society, recorded that "very extensive excavations have recently been discovered at the top and bottom of the Ajanta Pass. They have been very little visited on account of the difficulty of approaching them. The only information regarding them which I possess is contained in a memorandum of Captain Morgan's of the Madras Establishment, which states that they were described by the officers who visited them in 1819 as having seated figures with curled wigs. No traces of Brahmanical religion were discovered. The paintings were in a decent state of preservation." In 1824, James E. Alexander of the Lancers confirmed that the paintings were in "excellent preservation" but by the time Alexander's detailed description appeared in the *Transactions of the Royal Asiatic Society* in 1829 there were already visitors to Ajanta, among them Ralph, Gresley, and especially James Bird, who, inadvertently or intentionally, set the invaluable works of art on their career of effacement and disintegration. The gallery of despoilers of Ajanta also includes the "Curator" Narayan Ekenath, whose speciality was obliging tourists with souvenirs, amongst them a group of five male heads on a foot-square plaster which in 1922 was auctioned at Sotheby's in London and is now in the Boston Museum of Fine Arts.

In 1839, James Fergusson, one of the leading architectural historians of his day, while working on his outstanding paper, *The Rock-Cut Temples of India*, dispatched an urgent memorandum to the authorities, "to take steps to prevent further desecration and destruction of these venerable monuments of the past, and above all to appoint some one to make drawings of the fast perishing frescoes at Ajanta before decay and recklessness of the tourists have entirely obliterated them." As a result, an artist, the legendary Robert Gill, arrived at Ajanta in 1844 to copy the frescoes and subsequently, compelled by a strange inner urge, spent the best part of twenty-seven years painting and making sketches. But it was in vain, as almost all the facsimiles were destroyed by fire in 1866 while on loan to the Crystal Palace at Sydenham, outside London. Frustrated, worn out, but still defiant, Gill nevertheless continued to paint in the best tradition of the ancient Ajanta artists until he fell ill. He died at Bushawal, not far from Ajanta, where his tomb can still be seen. The mantle then fell on John Griffiths, who ten years later organized and led an expedition of students from the Bombay School of Arts. Again luck was against them, for eighty-seven of the hundred and twenty-five reproductions they made were ruined by fire in 1885 in the South Kensington Museum, London, where the collection was housed. Griffiths' indomitable students, however, succeeded in recopying sufficient paintings to enable him to bring out the first two volumes of reproductions to appear, entitled *The Paintings in the Buddhist Cave-Temples of Ajanta*. These were published in 1896-7 and, together with Lady Herringham's watercolour reproductions, *Ajanta Frescoes*, published in 1915, give a glimpse of what the painted walls looked like half a century ago. A standard of comparison is in fact provided by a more recently published work in four parts, *Ajanta*, produced by the then Government of Hyderabad in collaboration with the Oxford University Press, particularly as this monumental collection of plates was printed after the Italian experts Orsini and Cecconi had restored the paintings in 1920-21.

When I visited Ajanta in 1953, my fourth visit since 1947, it was against this background that I realized with startling excitement the existence of an enormous wealth of still surviving variations in colour and beautifully drawn sketches. These are either overlooked in the shadow of

THE MONKEY BENEATH A PALAS TREE. *Shaddanta Jataka.* Cave XVII, middle of 5th century

Plate 3

9

the luminescence of the overwhelming central figures (such as Bodhisattva Padmapani) or appear insignificant in the larger perspective of the fantastic world of Ajanta colour and design. Here variety is the key-note in a series of enlivening, lyrical drawings of humans, animals, birds and foliage, revealing moments when the artists were fully responsive to the picturesqueness of the incidents depicted and aware of the relationship between the hills and the trees and the flowers, between light and shadow. Searching in the most obscure corners of the caves, I noticed, for example, a lonely helpless bird gazing longingly at a distant narrow ray of sunlight; its value was recognized and *The Sacred Duck* has since become one of the favourite illustrations in *India: Paintings from the Ajanta Caves* in the UNESCO World Art Series, which I had the privilege to compile in 1954.

I hope that the selection of photographs in this volume collected in the course of my three subsequent visits, will attract no less attention. The relaxed, dignified calm of *The Monkey beneath a Palas Tree* (Pl. 3), consisting basically of one masterly sweep of a long stroke of the brush starting beneath the chin and forming a curve outlining the head and spine and terminating beneath the knee-cap, is a fine example of the translation of closely observed scenes and moments of action or repose into simple yet profoundly explicit drawings. A similar keenness of observation and drawing is seen in pictures such as *The Baby Elephant* (Pl. 5). In a similar style, the long flexible stroke of the brush which created the relaxed elegance of the two above-mentioned animals is also beautifully used in the drawing of *The Reclining Woman* (Pl. 33). The portrayal of the figure is clearly inspired by models of animal drawings, as contained in ancient *Sastras*, or guides to artistic practice. The tender, natural poise of the woman is compositionally balanced and supported by the curving of a single basic line, as if she were relaxing in a hammock. Her almost transparent garments, while preserving her modesty, clearly reveal that animal-like suppleness of the body and the limbs in which the Ajanta masters were so thoroughly proficient. *A Bikkshu with a Lotus* (Pl. 74) is another example in which the emphasis on essentials is achieved by combining rhythm and simple colour pattern. It is an excellent sketch drawn by an expert hand and coloured with only two tints, displaying all the basic elements of classical form. These qualities undoubtedly influenced the China of the T'ang dynasty, and its essentials are observed in Japan up to the coloured woodcuts of as late as the eighteenth and the nineteenth centuries. It is also noteworthy that in the portrayal of secular subjects, the master symbolists of Ajanta seem to have extended the domain of their sacred prerogative by creating a rare kind of metonymy in pictorial art, as in *Mithuna Figures* (Pl. 27), where an incredible *bhava-madhura* or tender feeling of reciprocal love and lovers' reunion is achieved by eschewing profane exhibitionism. The elegance of the contentment and modesty of the figures is stressed by diverting attention from even the facial expressions to the almost symbolic tenderness of the soft caress. With the same intention, as we are told in the *Vishnudharmottara*, moonlight is shown by a *kumada* flower in full bloom, and sunshine by drawing creatures and flowers suffering from and faded by the heat. The result is not merely exciting and effective but also subtle and expressive.

In the midst of a mass of figurative translations of feelings, sentiments and meanings, there are a few astonishingly unusual pieces. In this group is *The Courtier* (Pl. 22) which is effectively sidelighted in the manner of a Rembrandt or a Caravaggio by specks of yellow light used to infuse luminosity and a three-dimensional quality. This piece is a perfect illustration of the quotation in the *Mahayana Sutralamkara, citre . . . natonnatam nasti cam drsyate atha ca*, "there is no actual relief in the painting, and yet we see it there." In contrast is the conventional *animnonnata*, or flattened perspective of restricted tonal scale, as seen in *The Wailing Women* (Pl. 24), which has a remarkable parallel with the "cloisonnage" of Gauguin as it is produced by deeply demarcating plain surfaces of pure primary colours. Another interesting piece is *The Bodhisattva* (Pl. 67), conveying a curious Matisse-like movement by virtue of its unfinished character. Its summary technique and the method of overflowing colours beyond the borders of the undefined outlines of the hand and the Lotus is perhaps among the sources which inspired the art of our own time. In all these styles, however, whether the discerning observation of courtly life dramatically captured at the moment of action, the depiction of natural calamity, or the portrayal of the serenity of a holy life, the criteria are invariably vitality, unity and grace.

Recently, the Ajanta paintings have acquired a new complexion of delicate colour and intricate, extended tonal range as a result of the work carried out by the Government of India Archaeological Departments in removing the varnish misguidedly applied by the earlier restorers.

Plate 4   THE DOVE.   Cave II, end of 4th century

Plate 5   THE BABY ELEPHANT. *Shaddanta Jataka.*   Cave XVII, middle of 5th century

THE FIGHTING BULLS. Cave I, early 6th century

Plate 6

THE CALF. Cave VI, middle of 5th century

Plate 7

13

The cleaning of the yellowing and cracking patina has also revealed entirely new figures on some pieces of plaster where the gelatine was thickest. *The Calf* (Pl. 7), *The Supernatural Child Mahosadha* (Pl. 50) and *Sujata, the Farmer's Daughter* (Pl. 70) are good examples of paintings which have been redefined. This volume responds to the need to bring reproductions of these newly photographed masterpieces within reach of the art-loving public. Among the important paintings, I am particularly pleased to include the reproduction of the panel, *The Raja with his Retinue* (Pl. 48). It is one of the rare surviving masterpieces of the pre-Christian era, and a true understanding of the evolution in style that took place in the subsequent period is not possible without making some reference to it. The painting enshrines the pictorial manner as well as the social mood of the time. The reproduction is from an exact replica by the talented young artist G. C. Haloi, who spent more than six months at Ajanta painting this frieze. It was done at my request because the awkward position of the painting behind pillars and bad lighting conditions defeated all attempts at taking good photographs.

Among the landmarks in style, the Hinayana masterpiece (Pl. 48) and *The Dancing Girl with Musicians* (Pl. 47), the latter belonging to the Mahayana group, are the most significant. In the period of five hundred years which separates these two paintings, the few delicate and soft colours which so successfully created an atmosphere of a marvellous spontaneity in *The Raja with his Retinue* were replaced during the Mahayana period by elaborate sketches drawn in varying thickness of line and filled in with a variety of bright colours. The Mahayana piece, even if it displays an extraordinary breadth and confidence in draftsmanship, still betrays all the stresses and strains of an affected style which had been obviously improvised to meet the varied tastes of many different sections of the society. This is proved by an ancient Indian treatise of about the same period which states: "The masters praise the delineation and articulation of form, the connoisseurs praise the display of light and shade, women like the display of ornaments, and to the rest of the public richness of colours appeals." In this way, while the Mahayana painting obviously served its intended purpose of pleasing everybody, yet that unconcerned, uninhibited joy of the earlier period is sadly overshadowed by the melancholic realization that painting is now an escape from the inexorable realities of life into an artificially created and cultivated dream world of luxuries.

As an antithesis to the fundamental, cognitive nature of Ajanta art, I have also included a few frames of isolated colours and interrupted drawings which, more by accident than intent, seem to uncover, as it were, the original designs, and sparkle with the vitality that belongs to the line and colour alone. Distinct stages in the ancient technique of drawing and colouring are unfolded in particular in *The Three Ogresses* (Pl. 8). This picture reveals the basic rhythmic crescent-like short lines producing the enchanting effect of a swaying movement in the lower right-hand corner. The flexible lines are then lifted to another level, as a sequel to a circular composition, and are treated with the white washes of the intermediate stage. Finally, the painting is given finishing touches with the luminosity of the brilliant red colour which fills in the third figure at the top left-hand corner. In another painting, *A Pair of Antelopes* (Pl. 18), in which the finishing touches have completely disappeared, a fantastic effect is given by the accidental survival of patches of chalky white which appear to be suspended by a delightful arch of red against a graceful orange sketch of the wary animals.

These metaphors of abstract patterns, although they may be totally foreign to the finished paintings originally intended by the artists, have over the years cast an irresistible spell over me. Their fascination is so overwhelming that, even if it were possible, I would hesitate to recreate the elaboration of the freshly painted cave interiors of the olden days, whose atmosphere was akin to that of Bavarian churches. The newly cleaned bands of red, brown and black (Pl. 13) evoke a much more fundamental sense than the coincidental illusion of a painting by Rothko, because these colours were the first to be permitted in Buddhist monasteries. The ground was coloured black and the walls were treated with red chalk (*Vinaya Pitaka*). And the fragmentary patches of multi-coloured plaster in distorted shapes are as much an intimate, indissoluble part of the cave complex today as the streaks of soft mineral colours in the earth of Ajanta whence these colours were extracted. In any case, the reproduction of a few pictures, whose contents are valued only as a point of departure, is in no way intended to denigrate the ancient, perennial source of spiritual strength and the universal message inherent in the communicative nature of the creative genius of Ajanta. They merely provide a sidelight on some unusual areas of plaster before the curtain of decay and obliteration falls on this quaint and rather melodramatic aspect of the caves.

Plate 8

THE THREE OGRESSES. *Simhala Avadana*. Cave XVII, early 5th century

A Merchant in the Island of Ogresses. *Simhala Avadana.* Cave XVII, early 5th century

Plate 9

17

Plate 10   The approach to the caves from the source of the Waghora stream and the waterfalls called Sat Kund

A man continues to enjoy himself in paradise as long as his memory is green in the world; one should (therefore) set up a memorial on the mountain that will endure for as long as the moon and the sun shine.

Ajanta inscription in Cave XXVI

The Buddha was once staying at the squirrels' feeding place in the Bamboo Grove at Rajagriha. At that time lodgings had not been permitted to the monks by the Lord. So these monks wandered here and there and lived in a forest, at the root of a tree, on a hillside, in a glen, in a mountain cave, in a cemetery, or on a heap of straw in the open air. Now it so happened that a merchant of Rajagriha, realizing their plight, called on the monks and said: "If I, revered Sirs, were to have dwelling-places built, would you stay in my dwelling-places ?"

"Householder, dwelling-places have not been allowed by the Lord," replied the monks.

"Well then, revered Sirs, having inquired of the Lord, tell me (what he says)."

The monks agreed to do as the merchant of Rajagriha asked, and approached the Buddha respectfully and said: "Lord, the merchant of Rajagriha is anxious to have dwelling-places built. What line of conduct should we follow ?"

Then the Buddha, having given reasoned discourse, addressed the monks saying: "I allow, monks, five (kinds of) abodes: a dwelling-place, a curved house, a long house, a mansion and a cave." This is how the *Vinaya*, one of the three "baskets" of the Buddhist code of discipline, recorded the beginning of the merchants' patronage of the monasteries. It was then that the tradition was born.

At Pitalkhora and Kolhapur, archaeological finds of very early Buddhist relics reveal that small wandering groups of Buddhist Bhikshus (monks) had gained a foothold in the Deccan. They apparently chose the peaceful scarp of Ajanta as suitable for their monasteries because, apart from other considerations, it had the advantage of being near the flourishing trade centre of Paithan. This town, barely a hundred kilometers south of Ajanta, lay on the routes of rich merchants and traders travelling from the hinterland to the seaports north of Bombay, and through the three great passes leading out of the Deccan—the Bhor Ghat, the Nana Ghat and the Thal Ghat. The mercantile community, prospering on lucrative trade with the West, seems to have increasingly extended its patronage to the Buddhist monasteries, in much the same way as the Buddha's own favourite resort, the Jetavana monastery of Sravasti, was in fact donated by a wealthy merchant, Anathapindika. "Why should not a temple be raised by those possessing

wealth and desirous of mundane happiness as also of liberation," states an Ajanta record in Cave 11, "for happiness of the world as also for their own final emancipation?"

Based on the general Indian assumption that a holy life is led most easily in secluded and beautiful spots which give a feeling of repose and inspiration, the mountains came to be associated with the commemoration of religious ideals. The Buddha himself, so it is said, had withdrawn with his five disciples to Uruvela, "a pleasant spot and a beautiful forest," to enunciate his doctrine.

Thus in the tradition of the Master, the heart of the mountains called Sahyadri was well chosen for the establishment of the cave-temples. Also called the Ajanta chain, these mountains separate the valley of the river Tapti from that of the Godavari and form the northern wall of the Deccan table-land, the apex of which is covered by the forests of the Vindhya and Maikhal hills. The monasteries, scooped out of living rock at one of the Ghats that divide the table-land of the northern Deccan from Khandesh, belonged to a prominent *Janapada* named Bhogavardhana. The *Janapada* or "people's abode" was analogous to the "polis" or city-state of the Hellenic world. At the western edge of the plateau is a steep escarpment, where the western Ghat descends into a narrow picturesque strip of low country along the coast with sandy surf-bound beaches, rocky land and capes, fringed with swaying palm trees and rice fields. To the east, the isolated and sporadic peaks and ridges of the table-land lead on to a broad belt of plateau towards the east coast of India, separating the basin of the river Godavari from that of the Mahanadi, and finally merge into the eastern Ghats.

In contrast, during most of the year the arid landscapes in the vicinity of Ajanta roll towards the caves with an appalling monotony of sienna brown, broken only occasionally by the flashes of brilliant scarlet of the flame of the forest, the *palas* trees, or the blazing colours of the turbans and the saris of peasants working in the fields. Even in the welcome but short-lived rainy season, the refreshing greenery appears more of a camouflage than a reality. Then surprisingly, as if symbolic of the abruptness with which Ajanta emerges in the history of Indian archaeology of the second century BC and the chance discovery of the caves in the year 1819, a wonderful sight flashes into view with the first glimpse of the monasteries in the lonely, hidden ravine. From whichever direction one approaches the site, the enchantment is enhanced by the unexpectedness of meeting the wild semi-circular gorge, at one end of which the Waghora stream springs from its source, to flow in a series of waterfalls dropping as much as thirty meters. The shimmering water of the rivulet, as it emerges, cuts out seven peculiar bowls of rock called Sat Kund, then turns sharply to the left, carving the deep valley on the right into a long horse-shoe.

Embedded in the almost perpendicular cliff of solid rock, about eighty meters high, are the pillared and sculptured entrances to some thirty caves. The caves extend along a concave line running from east to west for about six hundred meters. The stream turns again at an acute angle towards the left around what appears to be an impasse, so that the road along the rocky bed of the Waghora, which approaches the caves from the other end, is unexpectedly terminated by a steep climb-up of dun coloured stones. A narrow pathway winds laboriously to the top and then suddenly leads into the remote historical past at the threshold of Cave 1, marking the beginning of the end of a tradition, the highest achievement of the Buddhist art of India, and a glorious chapter in the world history of wall-painting.

The Buddha's life and his teachings formed the central theme of the Ajanta art of painting; moreover, the colourful vibrations of that art's changing tempo, moods and style remained in faithful harmony with the later development of the religion. Siddhartha Gautama, the Buddha, son of a feudal chieftain of Kapilavastu, had rebelled at the age of twenty-nine against the misery and oppression which he saw about him, questioning the fundamental causes of the instability of human existence. He was born near Kapilavastu, while his mother Maya, the head wife of his father Suddhodana, was on her way to her parents' home. He was given the name Siddhartha at a great ceremony on the fifth day after his birth. When the soothsayers prophesied that he was destined to be either a Universal Emperor or a Universal Teacher, Suddhodana, to prevent the latter coming true, determined to bring up his son in delightful palaces where there was no sign of death, disease or misery. Gautama soon learned all the arts that a prince should know and, married his beautiful cousin Yasodhara, whom he won at a great traditional contest, putting to shame all his rivals, including his envious cousin Devadatta. But for all his success and prosperity,

Plate 12

Monks in a Monastery. Cave XVII, early 5th century

Gautama was not inwardly happy. The arrogance of lordly hierarchies, social inequalities and the persistence of pain which accompanies the human condition, caused a profound revulsion in him. Despite his father's efforts to interest him in secular affairs, his four Encounters—with age, sickness, death, and a wandering religious beggar with a countenance of inward peace and calm— decided his career.

There was a feast with dancing and music, rich food and much revelry on the fateful evening when the Buddha decided to become a mendicant. The agony of his separation, without saying farewell to his wife and their newly born son Rahula, becomes the theme of a most moving tale. When all were sleeping, Gautama roused Channa, his faithful groom, who saddled his favourite horse Kanthaka, and they quietly rode off into the night. Once away from the city, Gautama cut off his flowing hair, and stripped off his jewellery and his royal garments and sent them back to his father by the hand of Channa. This was the Great Renunciation.

For a time, Gautama's search for truth led him to become a disciple of two learned Brahman ascetics of Rajagriha, but though he concurred with their doctrine that man is born and reborn in this *samsara*, or universe, according to his *karma*, or deeds, their teachings did not satisfy him. The cure for the sorrows of the world, he thought, could not be found in the endless logomachies of the speculative believers, nor in the eternal cycle of births and rebirths. After some years of mental torment, self-flagellation, penance, austerity and fasting, the Buddha, now thirty-five years old, sat for forty-nine days beneath a large *bo* tree on the outskirts of the town of Buddh Gaya, and there obtained a glimpse into the true nature of man's predicament. This is known to Buddhists as the Great Enlightenment.

As the later version of the legend has it, Gautama was at first surrounded by hosts of gods and spirits, who fled as Mara, the spirit of sensual pleasures and worldly passion, approached the Buddha. For days Gautama withstood the temptations of all kinds contrived by Mara, who, first disguised as a messenger, told him that the Buddha's cousin Devadatta had revolted, thrown Suddhodana into prison and seized Yasodhara. Mara then called all his demon hosts and attacked the Buddha with whirlwind, tempest, flood and earthquake. The Lord of Temptation then called

Plate 13

A piece of freshly cleaned plaster in Cave XVII. Early 5th century

LEAVES AND FLOWERS. Cave 1, middle of 5th century

Plate 14

Figure 1

A Court Scene. *Simhala Avadana.* Cave xvii, early 5th century

his three most beautiful daughters, Desire, Pleasure and Passion, who danced and sang before Gautama and tried every means of seduction. But the Buddha was quite unmoved. This has been called the episode of the Temptation of the Buddha.

For another seven weeks he sat in the same spot to enjoy the bliss of deliverance and to envisage the whole universe as a system of law composed of struggling, striving creatures of all kinds, continually changing from one form of life into another. But against the concept of absorption into a possible Hindu Supreme God, the creator and organizer of the universe, he postulated the theory of deliverance from the interminable cycle of rebirths into the painless bliss of *nirvana,* or absolute emancipation. Prompted by a spiritual urge (somewhat similar to the *daimon* of Socrates) against withdrawal from life, he hastened to Benares where, in the Deer Park, he preached his First Sermon. The essence of this discourse, as it has come down to us, revolves around sorrow, the cause of which is desire; when desire is conquered it terminates the cycle of rebirths in *samsara,* and hence ends suffering. The way to salvation, the Buddha pointed out, is the eightfold righteousness : belief, resolve, speech, behaviour, occupation, effort, concentration and contemplation. And, to lead his followers to tread the eightfold path, the Master recommended

SIMHALA AVADANA

Formely known as the *Landing of Vijaya in Ceylon*, the imposing panel covering an entire wall in Cave XVII is now identified with the *Simhala Avadana*. Its grandiose composition has been compared by the Italian restorer Lorenzo Cecconi to the works of Venetian artists of the Renaissance.

Simhala was the accomplished son of a rich merchant, Simhaka. Despite his father's warning, he set out on a sea voyage in the company of five hundred other merchants. Simhaka's fears came true, for the ship, loaded with precious cargo, was wrecked and the merchants were cast ashore near a city of ogresses called Tamradvipa. These wicked, man-eating women lured on the merchants with their charms and devoured them all. Simhala himself however, was miraculously saved by the celestial white horse (the Bodhisattva) and was flown away to Jambudvipa. Later, an ogress who had earlier failed to entice Simhala, lured the king Simhakesari into admitting her to his harem, and eventually, with some of her friends, she devoured the king and all his family. Simhala then raised a powerful army, drove away the ogresses and colonized their island. Tamradvipa was thus renamed Simhaladvipa.

The brightly coloured scenes effectively portray the fantastic panorama of the shipwreck, the life of pleasure with the ogresses, the escape through the air on the back of the white horse, Balaha, the ogress's entry into the king of Simhakalpa's harem and the sad end of the king. All this, and the scenes depicting the expedition which the newly proclaimed king Simhala led against the ogresses to colonize their island epitomized the glorious ascendancy of the merchant class which patronized the Buddhist monasteries.

the six *paramitas*, namely virtue, morality, patience, hard work, meditation and wisdom. The Buddha differed from the prevalent philosophy in that he did not consider the *atman*, or self, as an entity, but as "a transitory manifestation of a collection of phenomena," so that what exists after death is not the self but *karma*, or the result of our deeds, and this can at last be extinguished by following the "middle path."

In a yellow robe and with an alms bowl in his hand, the Enlightened One travelled far and wide for forty-five years, showing the way to the annihilation of desire and the extinction of superficial pleasures. His message of forebearance, compassion and purity of the soul, refined by self-denial and austerity and advocated through gentleness and profundity of approach, converted his son, and later his wife, who became one of the first members of the order of Buddhist nuns. Many stories are told of his long years of preaching. Devadatta, his jealous cousin, tried unsuccessfully to kill Gautama by letting loose a mad elephant in his path. Gautama averted a war between his father's clan of Sakyas and the neighbouring tribe of the Koliyas by walking between the poised armies and convincing them of the futility and evils of bloodshed. He went alone to a notorious bandit, Angulimala, and converted him and his companions from their evil ways. Soon his magnificent and magnetic legend attracted people from all walks of life, in India and far beyond its boundaries, much like the development of the philosophy of Confucius in China (551-479 BC) and of the great Hebrew prophets who flourished in the years 750-500 BC. At the age of eighty, the Buddha approached the end of his journey in this world at Kusinagara. Having spent his last rainy season at Vaisali, he and his followers, while travelling northward, halted at Pava and were entertained by a lay worshipper, Cunda, who unknowingly offered them a meal of tainted pork. In consequence the Buddha fell ill and died that night under a *sal* tree. His last words were, "All composite things decay. Strive diligently!"

After the Buddha's death in the year 487 BC, a dispute arose over his remains, which were eventually distributed among his followers and enshrined in mounds called *stupas* or *dagobas*. The Master's teachings were consolidated for the benefit of posterity at the Satapani cave near Rajagriha, where five hundred disciples assembled to form the First Buddhist Council. The sacred books were classified in the Buddhist code of the three *Pitakas*, or "baskets," consisting of the *Vinaya*, the rules and discipline of the community; the *Sutras*, the collection of the Buddha's exposition of the doctrine, stories and sayings which largely make up the subject matter of the Ajanta painting; and the *Abhidharma*, a philosophical commentary on the faith. However, the accent on compassion, benevolence and generosity towards other people's views, and the absence of a central religious authority, inevitably produced in its wake contradictory ideas and divergent interpretations of the law, resulting in dissensions between various monasteries. In order to establish the unity of faith and purpose, a century later the Second Council was convened at Vaisali, but in vain. By the third century BC, there were over eighteen different sects, including the Vibhajyavadis who presumably compiled the orthodox Canon in the Pali language in Ceylon. The leaders of the other groups also established their own canons in Sanskrit. These were consolidated by the Emperor Asoka (circa 250 BC), who convened a Third Council in his capital, Pataliputra, where the "Excellent Law" was proclaimed.

The history of the Ajanta art of painting, or rather of Indian art in its Buddhist form, does not really commence until about three and a half centuries after the Buddha's lifetime. The missing links were perishable monuments, built of bamboo and wood, as these were the essential building material of the early Aryan settlers. This is proved by Pliny's reference to the "wooden town" in the Indus delta and Megasthenes' description of splendours which he witnessed in the "wooden palace" of the first Maurya Emperor, Chandra Gupta. They had a superstructure of trimmed timber set on a stylobate of stone, like the more primitive temples of Greece, and their replicas are to be seen today in the curvilinear roofs of the rock-cut caves. No wall-painting could exist before the use of stone comes into vogue. In any case, it is highly unlikely that the earlier iconoclastic attitude of the faith, with its injunctions against the sensuous appeal of objects expressed in colours and shapes, would have allowed much to be created which could be called specifically "Buddhist." All the arts, in fact, were considered an indulgence in the mundane life of luxury, so foreign to Buddhism; monks and nuns were forbidden to see the so-called "conversation pictures" or love scenes, which were at that time painted on the walls of royal chambers. In its characteristic

Plate 16

THE WOMAN WITH THE LOTUS. Cave 1, end of 6th century

A Queen in a Palace Scene. Cave 1, end of 6th century

6897

Plate 17

35

SIBI JATAKA

A hawk was once chasing a pigeon which, unable to escape from its enemy, took refuge with the king of the Sibis. The hawk demanded that King Sibi surrender the pigeon to him as it was his lawful prey. But the Bodhisattva replied, "He that gives up a frightened creature seeking protection from its foe, does not obtain help when he is himself in need. O Hawk! Let the people of Sibi's tribe place before thee a bull cooked with rice instead of this pigeon." The hawk refused and insisted on having the king's own flesh equal in weight to the pigeon's body. The Great Being, in order to redeem the life of the pigeon which in its dire distress had so confidingly taken refuge with him, cut pieces of flesh from his own body and gave them to the hawk and so saved the poor pigeon from death. Thus he was glorified in all the world throughout eternity.

Another version of the *Sibi Jataka* depicted at Ajanta narrates the King of Sibi's self-sacrifice after he had succeeded his father and become King of Arishtapura. He built six large alms-houses and visited them regularly to donate as much in alms as he could afford. One day, he proclaimed far and wide that "if there be any gift that I have never made—be it my eyes—I will gladly give it away." To test the king's resolve, the god Sakra, approached him in the guise of a blind beggar and asked him for the incredible gift. The Great Being gave away his eyes before the sorrowing ministers and wailing ladies of the court. Convinced of the Bodhisattva's unparalleled virtues, Sakra then restored his "eyes of Absolute Truth" to the king.

MRIGA JATAKA

The Great Being was once born as a beautiful deer with a shiny golden skin and a very melodious voice. One day, as he stood on the bank of the river Ganges admiring the colourful foliage of the trees and plants laden with fruits and flowers, he suddenly heard the cry of a drowning man. Regardless of his own safety, the Bodhisattva jumped into the water and dragged the man out of danger. This person was no other than the spoilt son of a rich merchant, who having squandered all his family's wealth had attempted suicide when approached by his creditors. Shaken with fright, the man promised not to speak to anyone of the incident nor to reveal the deer's abode. But when he returned home, he was told of the large reward which the King of Benares had offered to whoever should find the golden deer. The unscrupulous man, unable to resist the temptation of obtaining a richly caparisoned elephant and a golden casket containing a thousand pieces of money, broke his promise and revealed the place which the Bodhisattva frequented. The king spotted the animal, but as he was about to shoot the fatal arrow, the Bodhisattva checked him and in his sweet voice narrated the story of how he had rescued the ungrateful man. The king wished to punish the informer but the Bodhisattva intervened and asked the king to pardon him. The monarch then invited the virtuous deer to his capital where the queen, the courtiers and the king's subjects were all enthralled by the Bodhisattva's wisdom. As a favour, the king then proclaimed that "he would give protection to all creatures and no one could hurt a beast or a bird in his kingdom."

Plate 18

A Pair of Antelopes. *Mriga Jataka.* Cave XVII, early 5th century

A Forest Scene. *Mriga Jataka*. Cave XVII, early 5th century

Plate 19

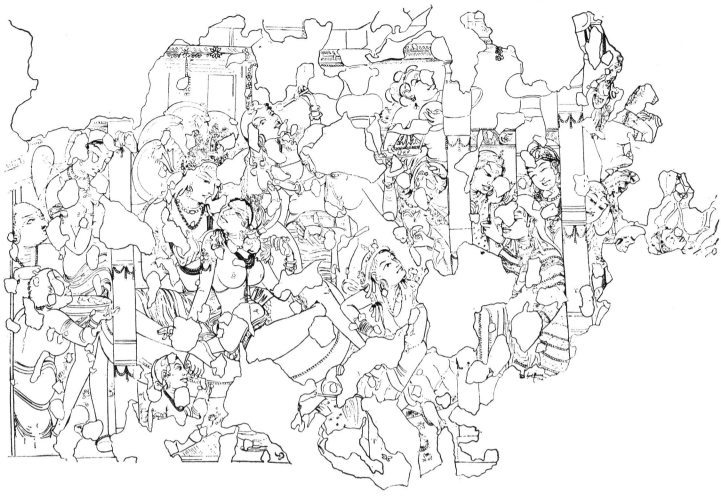

Figure 2

style, the *Vinaya* states: "Once the group of six monks had a bold design made with the figures of women, figures of men, in a dwelling-place. People who saw the pictures said: 'Like house-holders who enjoy pleasures of the senses.' This matter was brought to the notice of the Buddha who said: 'Monks, you should not have a bold design made with figures of women, figures of men. I allow, monks, only wreath-work, creeper work, swordfish teeth, the five strips (of cloth design).'"

For a considerable time the essential Indian tradition of non-representational art, using only geometrical symbols as supports of contemplation, was maintained. But this form of self-denial was too abstract a concept to survive for ever among the monks or to be accepted by the laity, who were all steeped in the popular folk art of the common people. The need for a representational art thus grew organically from the spread of the order, and Buddhist puritanism gave way step by step to popular taste.

MAHAJANAKA JATAKA

Aritthajanaka and Polajanaka were the two sons of King Mahajanaka of Mithila. Afther Mahajanaka's death, Aritthajanaka ascended the throne and offered the viceroyalty to his younger brother. One day a slave told the king that the viceroy had secret plans to kill him and usurp the throne. Aritthajanaka became suspicious and had Polajanaka arrested and thrown into prison. But because Polajanaka was innocent, the gods let him escape. In the course of time, having become master of the frontier districts, the younger brother assembled a powerful army and sent an ultimatum to the king saying, "I was not your enemy before but I am indeed your enemy now; give the royal umbrella up to me or give battle." In the battle that followed, Aritthajanaka was killed and his pregnant queen fled the palace in disguise. She took refuge in the city of Champa, where she brought forth a son who was called Mahajanaka after his grandfather. The prince grew up to be a handsome and learned man and when he discovered who his real father was, he asked his mother "Have you any money? If not, I shall become a merchant trader in order to make money and seize my father's kingdom." Later, Mahajanaka with a few other merchants sailed for Suvannabhumi. Unfortunately the ship was wrecked but Mahajanaka was miraculously saved by the daughter of the gods, Manimekhala, and was taken to the city of Mithila. Meanwhile King Polajanaka had died without leaving any male heir and had willed that his kingdom should go to the person "who can please the princess, my daughter Sivali, or who knows which is the head of a square bed, or who can string the bow which requires the strength of a thousand men, or who can draw out the sixteen great treasures." Where others failed, Mahajanaka succeeded, and so became King of Mithila and married the beautiful Savila. However, the pomp and luxuries of royal life did not attract the Bodhisattva so that by and by he renounced his kingdom to become an ascetic.

Later, Asoka's royal patronage of Buddhism seems to have encouraged further modification of the rules. The ignominy implicit in representational art began to decrease, and echoes started to resound from the art tradition of the Indus Valley civilization which had flourished during the later part of the third millennium BC. These art forms consisted of seals, tablets and other artifacts representing animal figures, such as tigers, buffaloes, crocodiles, elephants, deer and even multi-headed monsters, hybrid creatures, and trees and flowers. The ubiquitous lotus in the hair of the Mohenjo-Daro goddess (the Magna Mater of Antiquity) reappears here to indicate the presence of the Buddha and the Great Enlightenment in the same way as the primeval tree worship of ancient India is replaced by the worship of the Bodhi tree or Tree of Wisdom at Buddh Gaya. Sanctity is likewise bestowed on the Lumbini garden with its *sal* trees at Kapilavastu, where the Buddha was born, the Deer Park near Benares, where he preached his First Sermon, and the grove near Kusinagara, where he achieved his *nirvana*. The canon against representing the person of the Buddha, a taboo which is observed until the first century AD, encouraged the rendering of Bodhisattvas as animals in the same way as the main events of the Master's life are represented by symbols borrowed from animistic nature cults. The elephant, the horse and the deer stood respectively for the Conception, the Great Renunciation and the First Sermon. Gradually the patrons and craftsmen enlarged the area of their prerogative by depicting human forms adorned with ornaments, despite the severity of Hinayana convention which proscribed hedonistic evasion. This advance probably followed a period of intense disputation, somewhat similar to the Iconoclastic Controversy which retarded the progress of Byzantine art in Europe. In this way, for example, the image of the lotus goddess on Basarh terracottas was transformed into the goddess Padmapriya, "to whom the lotus is dear," as seen on Buddhist monuments. The sensuous moon-shaped breasts resting on the narrow waists of dryads with heavy hips, and the nature spirits which acted as guardians of Buddhist shrines, both enrolled from the forests of the pagan world, were no longer a blasphemy. With the passage of time other representational forms were assimilated, such as *yaksha* kings who ruled the four quarters, *nagas* or serpent kings of the waters, the fabulous *kinnaras* or musicians, the *gandharvas* and *apsarasas*, the earth and mother goddesses and divinities of fertility.

44

The appearance of human forms in art did not, however, take precedence over the depiction of non-human life, so that the general concept of style and approach to colouring continued uninterrupted. In fact, the colourful luxuriance of tropical trees and flowers associated with major holy events in the life story of the Buddha, and the graceful elegance of animals and birds embodying all the virtues of Bodhisattvas, continued to be considered in an absolute sense much more beautiful than the imperfect human models. The ancient *sastras*, or guides to artistic practice containing rules of drawing and proportion and other data of a technical nature, while emphasizing the symbolic rather than the realistic approach to the portrayal of the divine beings, compare their anatomy to flowers and animals. The human torso is metaphorically described as the subtle body of a lion, the arms as the flexible tapering trunk of an elephant, hanging from the shoulders which resemble the animal's smooth round head. The emphasis on the intrinsic beauty of animal drawing is obvious, for example, from the procedure which is laid down in the *Sukranitisara* of Sukracarya. This medieval text states that "when a figure of a horse is to be made, the model should always be in view, and if one cannot be looked at, the figure should not be drawn. The artist having made his visual contemplation of the horse and being attentive to its forms should do his work embodying all its proportions."

In the language of art the Indus Valley tradition is echoed throughout every stage of evolution of the Ajanta style. It is reflected in the plastic vigour of animal drawings in the early pictures, which are infused with the majestic aloofness and dynamic realism of the bull on a famous Mohenjo-Daro seal, and the animals and birds on steatite seals, and other terracottas of about the same period recently discovered at Kalibangan in Rajasthan. The tradition survived even later with remarkable continuity. For instance, *The Monkey beneath a Palas Tree* (Pl. 3) as compared with the same animal on an ancient Harappa seal is a notable example of sculpture being literally translated into painting, just as the robust forcefulness of a freshly recovered terracotta bull from Kalibangan has its undeniable imprint on *The Fighting Bulls* (Pl. 6). In the depiction of the human figures, too, an astonishing feeling for plastic volume and a remarkable emphasis on the essentials bring to mind such examples of Indus valley figurines as the red sandstone torso of

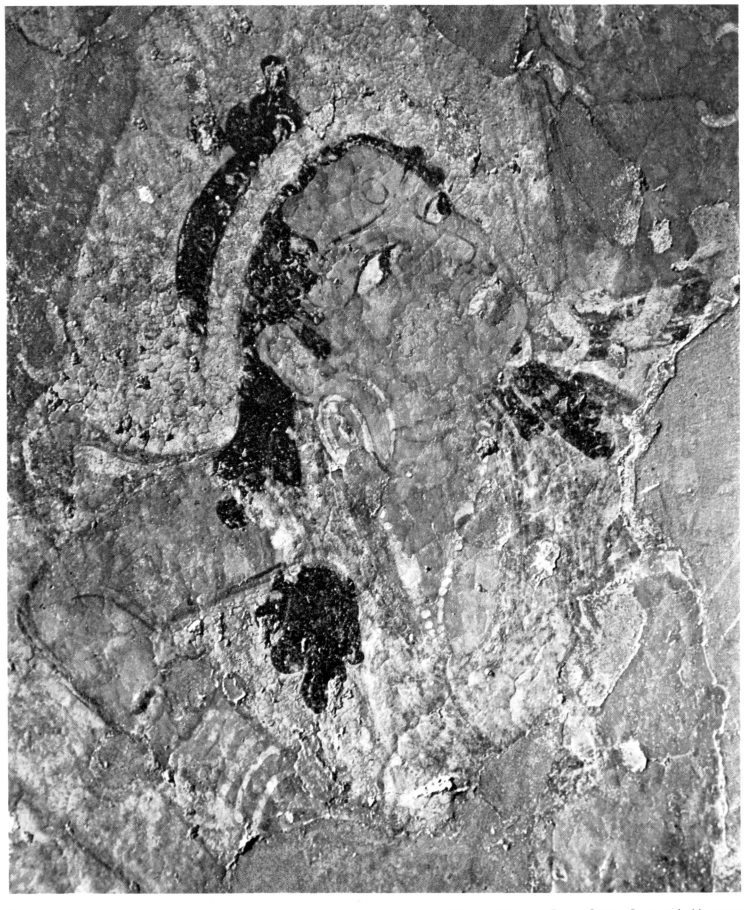

Plate 21

A Dancing Girl in a Palace Scene. Cave 1, early 6th century

THE COURTIER. *Vishvantara Jataka*. Cave XVII, early 5th century

Plate 22

Figure 3   SYAMA JATAKA. First Episode. Cave x, first half of 1st century BC

a male, now in the National Museum, New Delhi. Also carried down from antiquity are the fabulous, highly coloured episodes of the Buddha's life as told by his followers, and the *Jatakas*, or birth legends, tales supposedly about the Master's previous lives. The great white elephant with a lotus flower in his trunk, which approached Maya, Gautama's mother, and entered her side while she was carried away in her dream to the divine lake Anavattapa in the Himalayas, already had a place in Indian mythology, suggesting that the origin of the caryatids of the universe sprang from the churning of the Ocean of Milk. The fecund, imaginative genius of these unsurpassed story-tellers of ancient India had, both in prose and in verse, an enormous treasury of fables and parables, and heroic tales of adventure, endurance and sacrifice, with a varied cast of kings, common folk and ascetics, hunters and merchants. They also told tales of birds and animals. These stories are now identified by Buddhists with the names of the people known to the Buddha, while the hero of these fantastic anecdotes is deemed to be the Bodhisattva. The favourite version of *Sibi Jataka* depicted at Ajanta is obviously derived from the *Mahabharata*, where Indra and Agni assume the forms of the hawk and the pigeon to test the righteousness of Prince Sibi, who is now no other than the Bodhisattva. The term Bodhisattva, which in its simplest meaning implies the one striving for and capable of supreme knowledge of Buddhahood (like Gautama himself before he attained enlightenment), is lavishly applied to the mythical birds and animals

48

SYAMA JATAKA. Second Episode. Cave x, first half of 1st century BC   Figure 4

of the *Jataka* stories, especially during the early phase of the religion. These archangels of the animistic cults freely roam in the world of mankind to set examples by their deeds of self-sacrifice and thus show the path to salvation.

In this way, enriched by the vivid legends of the Buddha's life contained in the monumental collection of five hundred and forty-seven *Jatakas*, and stimulated by the adaptation of the folk and animistic motifs, the major characteristics of Ajanta painting began to come into focus in the late pre-Christian era. The two elements succeeded in merging the colourful fantasies of pagan passions and delights with contrasting religious reverence, thus introducing the basic tradition of the narrative art. With little decorative embellishment, the stress on the ultimate spiritual significance imparted, in a developing art, that particular quality assigned not so much to acute observation from without, but to a deep sense of kinship with all human and non-human life from within. As colours and shapes took on deeper meanings of canonical attitudes to suit the requirements of a higher ideal, intelligibility progressively depended not only on recognition but also on legibility on a metaphysical level.

From its very inception at Ajanta, *citrabhasa* or painting, is regarded as a kind of solid representation; a monk *vutthapeti*, "raises," a picture (*vinaya*), or a painter *samutthapeti*, "raises up," a shape on a wall surface by means of his brush and colours (*samyutta nikaya*). This was in a way

Plate 23   THE CHAURI BEARER. In a scene commonly known as The Persian Embassy. Cave 1, 7th century (?)

THE WAILING WOMEN. *Sibi Jataka*. Cave 1, early 6th century

Plate 24

inevitable, as the art of painting evidently came into its own during the phase of development when sculpture in the round, as reliefs flattened out on the railings and walls of Buddhist monuments, began to be covered with layers of bright colours to enliven the dull surfaces of stone. Whether it was reliefs in stone which laid the foundation for the technique of producing relief effect in colours by shading, or whether the transition from sculpture in the round to relief carving was in fact inspired by the lead given by the painters, it is difficult to tell. But the artists working on these decorations were undoubtedly aware of, if not proficient in, both media. The approach was almost identical; the stone was chiselled into relief with the figures emerging to a middle distance against a background, while the painting was "raised" on the wall surface by means of colouring and shading. The rules for painting were also valid for sculpture. In the study of the evolution of style in Ajanta, this factor of interdependence between painting and sculpture is of considerable importance, as the gaps in our knowledge created by the destruction of painted surfaces can be filled by proxy by studying contemporary pieces of sculpture in neighbouring cultural centres with which Ajanta artists were then in contact.

The sense of volume is obvious in the fragments of drawings depicting the *Syama Jataka* (late second century BC) and *Shaddanta Jataka* (late first century BC) on the right wall of Cave x and the painting on the opposite wall, *The Raja with his Retinue* (Pl. 48) of half a century earlier. Through the soft hues of a few colours, red ochre, yellow ochre, *terra verde*, lampblack and lime white, the grief of the blind parents of Syama at his tragic death from an arrow shot by the Raja of Benares, and Queen Subhadra's fainting at the sight of the tusks in the *Shaddanta Jataka*, are forcibly expressed in a style closely related to the contemporary sculpture in the round and in relief. The restrained power, serenity and elegance of the red stone torsos of ancient Harappa are reflected here in long, bold and vigorous curves drawn with great precision in a line of unvarying thickness, showing dexterity of drawing and expression. In terms of style, however, the main features resemble more the manner found at the great Buddhist shrine of Sanchi. The costumes, the "veils" over the women's heads and the architecture depicted are typical of Sanchi sculptures of the first century BC. Their purity is found in the frieze (Pl. 48) where the Raja, identified as

Nagaraja, with his retinue of soldiers and ladies is approaching the Bodhi tree. This frieze, like the others belonging to the pre-Christian era in Caves IX and X, almost certainly found a place within the orbit of the classical monuments of early Andhra art. These are painted longitudinally in narrow horizontal panels. The scenes unfolding on a ribbon-like space on the walls are not sub-divided as in the later period except for an occasional tree, or a building or a group of rocks, which vaguely defines the end of one scene and the beginning of another. The rationality of composition is in tune with the depiction of figures which are generally drawn in rows at one or two levels, but not more. The personages are painted in dark brown or burnt sienna, and display the round faces with small bright eyes, short pointed noses, narrow mouths and full lips of southern types. Cave IX is regarded as somewhat older than Cave X; the latter, as a result of the palaeographic analysis of an important inscription, is placed in the second century BC. But as can be expected, this does not bear much relation to the dates of the paintings because quite a number were added at widely different periods. The beautiful portrait of *Gautama, the Buddha* (Pl. I) painted on a pillar in Cave X is assigned to a period as late as the fifth century. Similarly, paintings in Cave IX such as *Nagaraja with Attendants, A Group of Votaries approaching a Stupa*, and *The Buddha with a Group of Votaries*, are more akin to the reliefs of the famous stupa of Bharhut and are considered, to be an offshoot of Sunga art.

Unfortunately, at Ajanta little remains of the painted surfaces to display the development of style so as to match step by step the fascinating record of evolving movement which can be seen in the contemporary sculptures of other Indian centres. Nevertheless, the few remnants of these paintings leave little doubt that the Ajanta painters of the pre-Christian period were certainly better than their colleagues, the sculptors of Bharhut and early Sanchi. Although created at about the same time, the flow of line portraying feminine grace, tenderness and animation of the group of women on their way to worship the Bodhi tree in *The Raja with his Retinue* is years in advance of the earliest Yakshas and Yakshis carved on the stupa of Bharhut. Even the famous wood nymphs of the archaic sculpture on the railing of the stupa, which belong to the end of the first century BC and are known for their charm as they entwine themselves around the trunks of trees,

Plate 25

BODHISATTVA PADMAPANI. Cave 1, second half of 6th century

BODHISATTVA AVALOKITESVARA. Cave 1, second half of 6th century

Plate 26

55

KSHANTIVADI JATAKA

Once when the King Kalabu reigned in Benares, the Bodhisattva was born in a wealthy Brahmin family. He was given the name of Kundaka-kumara, and when he came to age his parents provided him with a comfortable house and also gave him all the fortunes of the family. But when his father and mother died, the Bodhisattva was stricken with grief and he decided to become an ascetic. Therefore, he distributed all his wealth in alms among deserving people and left for the Himalayan regions where he lived on wild fruits. Once, when Kundakakumara came to Benares to collect some salt and vinegar, he sat down to rest under a tree in the Royal Park. Coincidently the same day, King Kalabu, accompanied by ladies of the court also came to the park to watch a dance performance. He soon became intoxicated with alcohol, and fell asleep during the show by laying his head in the lap of a favourite concubine; and the dancing girls finding the King asleep, abandoned their instruments and went strolling in the park. Thus they met the ascetic and surrounded him to listen to his wise discourse. Meanwhile the King woke up and being told where the dancing girls had gone, rushed with the sword in his hand to the ascetic and demanded to know what he was preaching. The Bodhisattva replied, "the doctrine of peace." Thereupon the tyrant summoned his executioner and ordered him to torture Kundakakumara with a lash of thorns and whip him with two thousand strokes. As the Bodhisattva's spirit still remained unshaken, the cruel King ordered to cut the ascetic's hands, feet, nose and ears. Yet the Great Being remained calm and devotedly repeated his wise words until he lost consciousness. Finally, the King struck the Bodhisattva above the heart with his foot and departed in rage; but as he left the park the mighty earth split in two and a flame issued forth which enveloped the King and sank into the earth. The Bodhisattva died, but it is said that the people of Benares saw him rise again and walk back to the Himalayas.

CAMPEYYA JATAKA

The Bodhisattva was once born in a poor family and greatly coveted the glories and wealth of the serpent King Campeyya. Thus in his next life he was born in a snake's body. He lived comfortably in the Naga world but was discontented and even attempted to take his life. His beautiful wife Sumana helped him to revive his interest in life and was his constant companion. On one occasion when the Bodhisattva was going across the highway, he was caught by a young Brahmin of Benares. The cruel man mistreated him and compelled him to learn the art of dancing. Soon the fame of the dancing snake spread far and wide so that the King Uggasena of Benares also sent for the Brahmin. The King arranged a magnificient show in his palace which was attended by thousands of people. Meanwhile, Sumana having missed her consort, went out in search and finally found the Great Being in the King's palace. She approached the King and asked for mercy; and the benevolent monarch, touched by Sumana's devotion at once ordered the snake to be set free. The Bodhisattva and his consort who miraculously re-appeared as a young man and a beautiful woman, then invited the King to share the luxuries of the Naga Kingdom. The King thus realised that the snake was no other than the serpent King Campeyya, who lived in the river Campa, flowing between the hostile Kingdoms of Anga and Magadha. Earlier, in one of the battles between the armies of the two Kings, the Magadha King was defeated; and as he was being pursued by Anga's warriors he jumped into the river Campa and would have drowned had he not been saved by Campeyya. The Naga King had then invited the Magadha King to his jewelled pavilion and the two became fast friends. Subsequently Campeyya helped his friend with his great powers to vanquish Anga and thus proclaimed the King of Magadha to be the sovereign of both the Kingdoms. In this way the tradition was born by which the Kings of Magadha annually erected a jewelled pavilion on the bank of the river Campa, and all the people beheld the glory of the Bodhisattva.

Plate 27

MITHUNA FIGURES. Cave 1, second half of 6th century

THE PRINCE AND HIS CONSORT. *Sibi Jataka*. Cave 1, early 6th century

Plate 28

Figure 5   A Group of Votaries approaching a Stupa. Cave IX, 1st century BC

do not attain the elegance of the dancers. If we compare, say, the well-known wood nymphs standing on their "vehicles" with the principal dancer of the frieze in Cave x, we find there are some remarkable points of similarity; they are each portrayed with one arm looped so that the hand rests on the curved hips, while the other arm is outstretched well above the head, and in both cases they have beautifully moulded figures with bare round breasts. Yet the graceful and vibrant swaying movement of the Ajanta dancer with an enchanting tilt of the head and the slanting look in the direction she is moving is very different from the comparative rigidity of the wood nymphs. The Ajanta figures were already moving away from certain features of archaic art, such as complete frontality and symmetrical immobility, at a time when sculpture in relief was still struggling to get out of the static mould. It seems that the earliest existing examples of Ajanta painting cannot be classified as archaic in the strictest sense of the word, since they have already entered the transitional period which was to carry them on to the classical phase—a maturity which marks the emergence of creative works from the prehistoric world into the conscious affirmation of history. The subtle, beautifully drawn sketches effectively portraying the pose and gestures of the human figure and the grandeur of trees and flowers could not have been done by artists who were not supreme masters of their medium. They were perhaps in the vanguard of the aesthetic movement and therefore in advance of their time.

The maturity of specialization is observed also in the preparation of the surface on which the colours are laid. The general principles of the technique were evidently known from early times. In the "Cullavagga" section of *Vinaya Pitaka* it is stated that the Master, when approached by the monks, said : "I allow, monks, whitewash, black colouring, red chalk (to be used) in a dwelling-place." But as the red chalk would not adhere to the rough walls, the Master permitted

the use of such binding media as the red powder of rice husks mixed with clay, mustard powder, oil of beeswax and the excrement of earthworms, and further allowed these to be sponged over with a piece of cloth.

In the period of two or three hundred years which preceded the earliest stone monasteries, much must have happened in the field of colouring and drawing to necessitate changes also in the technique of surface preparation. In the cave-temples the rough surface of the naked stone walls was first covered with a layer of potter's clay taken from the slimy beds of pools and mixed with molasses, bdellium and rice husks, with perhaps animal glue as a binding medium. On this a thin layer of lime plaster was applied as priming. The chapters dealing with painting in the *Vishnudhar-mottara*, probably compiled during the seventh century but containing information from earlier times, give details of the ingredients of *rinzafo* (clay plaster) which show that it corresponded roughly with the material used at Ajanta. A buffalo skin was boiled in water until it became soft. Sticks were then made of the paste and dried in the sunshine. It is stated that if colour is mixed with this hard plaster, called *vajralepa*, it makes it fast, and if white mud is mixed with it, it serves as a perfect medium for coating the walls. *Vajralepa* coating was usually done in three layers over a plaster which consisted of powdered brick, burnt conches and sand, mixed with a liquid prepa-ration of molasses and drops of a decoction of *mudga* (*phaseolus munga*). To this a quantity of mashed ripe bananas or tree raisins and the pulp of Bell fruit (*aeglemarmelos*) was also added. After the mixture had dried it was again ground down and mixed with molasses and water until it became soft. The wall surface was washed down with water until it was thoroughly clean, and then the plaster was applied with a spoon. This was the twofold process by which the wall was prepared for painting. A preliminary sketch in haematite was drawn on the surface while it was still slightly

Plate 29   Right-hand corridor leading to the Hariti Shrine in Cave II

A Monastery. Cave XVII, early 5th century

Plate 30

wet, followed by an under-painting in grey or white monochrome, like the medieval Italian practice of *terra verde*. The recent revelation of the depth to which the pigments are absorbed in the nearly two centimetre thick plaster has confirmed the view that the application of mineral colours on a semi-wet surface, instead of a completely dry plaster, was a technique already known to Ajanta painters. On this surface an outline in cinnabar red was filled in with various colours, proceeding from under-painting as the base to the appropriate colours of the subject. Finally, when dry the semi-fresco was finished off with a dark outline for final definition and a burnishing process to give lustre to the surface. Even in the earliest caves the "Eight Limbs" of the *Samaranganasutradhara* were apparently known. These were : *vartika* (the crayon), *bhumibandhana* (preparation of the surface), *rekha-karma* (outline work), *laksana* (the characteristic lineaments of types), *varnakarma* (colouring), *vartana-karma* (plastic modelling or relief by shading), *lekha-karma* (correction) and *dvika-karma* (final outline).

The impact of the "Excellent Law" propagated by the missionary zeal of Asoka gradually faded in the Indian subcontinent, mainly due to the revival of Brahmanism and dissensions among the various monasteries. Schism also occurred between the Ceylon Buddhists, who wished to hold fast to the formulations of the Third Council securely established in 242 BC by Mahindra, the Emperor's son, and now called Hinayana, or Small Vehicle, and the eighteen other sects of North India who accepted a new draft of canon called the Mahayana, or Great Vehicle. The latter was sanctified in the Fourth Council called by the Kushan Emperor Kanishka, probably in AD 100. The new canon, while retaining most of all that Hinayana stood for, in addition absorbed certain metaphysical formulae, magical dissertations, chants and incantations which were common among the lower classes of society. The absence of examples has deprived us of a full understanding of the successive styles of Ajanta painting in the long interlude of nearly five centuries between the Hinayana and the Mahayana groups, but undoubtedly the changing concepts were in no small measure inspired by the rapidly evolving Mahayana sense of absolute idealism. Nagarjuna and Aryadeva, the two great Buddhist philosophers in the second and third centuries respectively, built the subtle system of Madhyamika Mahayana by deriving much of their metaphysical formulations from the passionate, mystical and lyrical moods in the worship of the Hindu gods. They seem, as a result, to have provided the artists with more freedom to paint the doctrine of the Buddha, coloured by the fantasies of Hindu iconography. While Nagarjuna founded the Madhyamika school, Ashvaghosha wrote the most outstanding epic on the life of the Buddha, *Buddhacharita*, the poetic treatment of which greatly facilitated the change-over to the new ideals. In these the Buddha ceased to be a dead teacher and became instead a saviour-god made incarnate for the salvation of the human race. Accordingly, an inscription in Cave XVI states : "Victorious is the Muni (Buddha) who won complete victory over death and attained the state where one neither decays nor dies; and who, even though he has entered *nirvana*—that state of utter calm and bliss, beyond fear and void of locality—fulfils the desires of all beings." The historical figure of Gautama became eternal and absolute in the Yogachara doctrine, whose greatest exponent, the Buddhist monk Asanga, is said to have lived for some time at Ajanta. The theory of avatars, the god-representatives of Vaishnavite Hinduism and Jainism, was adopted and the Buddha became the latest in the series of incarnations of the Adi-Buddha, or primeval spirit. The Bodhisattva ideal is first encountered in early Mahayana sutras such as the *Saddharma Pundarika*, compiled sometime in the second century AD. As a result of this, devotion to a code of ethics was gradually replaced by personal devotion. This produced an antithesis to the Hinayana austerities in the domain of art, so that the innocent and essentially simple manner of telling the story of Buddhism through symbols was relaxed. Following the concept of the image of the Buddha, which probably originated in the first century AD, the interpretation of spiritual law through symbols was largely superseded by the realistic human forms of the inmates of the Buddha's paradise : Avalokitesvara, Amitabha, Maitreya and many other supra-terrestial saviours. These were late additions to the Buddhist pantheon. Like the saints and madonnas of medieval Christianity, these ambassadors of Mahayana Buddhism acquired a sanctity of their own, as compared with the Hinayana Bodhisattvas, by eternally renouncing the attainment of Buddha-hood in order to remedy the sorrows and the agonies of suffering humanity. In this manner, the fresh ideas and ideals of the creative period of Mahayana prompted the inhabitants of Ajanta to

Plate 31

Votaries with Offerings. Cave 11, end of 4th century

VOTARIES WITH OFFERINGS. Cave II, end of 4th century

Plate 32

SYAMA JATAKA

Dukulaka and his wife Parika belonged to the Hunters' tribes that dwelt not far from Benares, on the bank of the river Ganges. The couple having renounced the worldly life were living as anchorites when they were miraculously blessed with a son (the Bodhisattva), who was named Suvanna Syama. Unfortunately, as a result of a sin committed in their former lives, both the parents were blinded by a snake when during a storm they were seeking shelter under a tree. Thus they became entirely dependent on their son who in turn selflessly offered to devote all his life looking after them. Accompanied by friendly deers, he collected fruits and flowers from the forest everyday and fetched water from the river. Now it so happened that King Piliyakkha of Benares who, because of his lust for venison had entrusted the Kingdom to his mother, came to this region for a deer hunt. He erected a shelter on the bank of the river Migasammata and lay in ambush. In the morning Syama came to bathe in the river, and as usual had put on his bark garment and a deer's skin over his shoulder. The King, not knowing if Syama was a human or a devil hit him with a poisoned arrow. Fatally wounded, Syama fell on the ground facing the direction of his parent's hut and said, "I have no enemies, and I have enemity against none; alas, who will now take care of my poor parents ?" The King realising that he had shot an innocent man who disregarding his personal safety was thinking only of his parents, was stricken with remorse. He, therefore repented and promised the dying Bodhisattva that he would take care of Syama's parents as he would of his own. Meanwhile the daughter of the Gods Bahusodari who watched the incident from the Gandhamadhana mountain descended on the scene. By her supernatural powers she then restored the life to Bodhisattva and also blessed the blind parents so that they regained their eye-sight. The King then accepted the Law of the Buddha and proclaimed that no one in his Kingdom could take the life of a man, beast or bird.

VISHVANTARA JATAKA

Prince Vishvantara who lived in the city of Jetuttara was the son of King Sanjaya and his chief consort Phusati. Long before the Bodhisattva's birth fortune-tellers had predicted that Vishvantara's whole life shall be devoted to almsgiving. Accordingly, soon after his birth he held out his hand to his mother and said, "I wish to make some gift, please give me something" ; and Phusati gave him a purse of money to donate. At the age of eight years, he offered to give away even his heart, his flesh or his eyes, and his fame spread far and wide in the Kingdom of Sibi. Now at that time the neighbouring Kingdom of Kalinga was stricken with drought and famine. To help the suffering population, Vishvantara, against the wishes of his people gave away his precious white elephant, which had the magical quality of drawing rain. The citizens of Jetuttara protested and threatened revolt so that to save Vishvantara's life, his father was compelled to banish him. Even in difficult conditions of exile where he was accompanied by his wife Madri and their two children Prince Jali and Princess Kanhajina, Vishvantara was undaunted in his resolve; to four Brahmins, who had not shared any gift, he gave away the horses and the chariot, obliging the family to go on foot. Yet Vishvantara's ordeal was not over and the Gods to test his virtues, even allowed his children to be kidnapped by a cruel Brahmin Jujeka. He fled with the children, bound and beat them, and at night he left them lying on the ground while he climbed up the trees for fear of wild beasts. The Gods, however, protected Jali and Kanhajina and tended and fed them every night in guise of their parents; and finally helped the children by misleading Jujeka to the city of Jetuttara while he intended to seek refuge in Kalinga. Thus the people of Kalinga having recognised the children brought them to Sanjaya's court. The virtues of their parents also having been established, the couple was summoned by Sanjaya and Phusati from their hermitage and were restored to their children amidst royal honours.

Plate 33

THE RECLINING WOMAN. Cave 1, early 6th century

WOMEN ON THE BALCONY. Cave II, 5th century

Plate 34

introduce images of the Buddha in the new caves and also in the earlier Hinayana ones, and, what was more radical, to depict the *saktis* of the Bodhisattvas, which are the Buddhist counterpart of the female aspects of the Hindu gods.

The transition in the Buddhist philosophical thought was in particular provoked by an emergent mercantile community enjoying unprecedented prosperity, whose new ideas of modern civilization, traded in by way of the Indian west coast, interacted with assiduously held traditional values. There are a number of eulogies inscribed in the caves in praise of the prosperous donors and even such inscriptions which do not mention names were obviously intended to flatter the vanity of the patrons. An inscription in Cave XXII below a seated figure of the Buddha asserts : "Those who erect an image of Jina (the Buddha) become endowed with *good looks, good fortune* and *good qualities*, acquiring resplendent brightness and insight." Contact with the West and rising standards of living infused a *joie de vivre* into art at a critical time when the ceaseless repetition of formulae by artisans trained by precept and pattern-books had eroded the earlier originality and sureness of vision. The policy of the Roman Empire during the first two centuries aimed at increasing trade with India by the direct sea route and received a great impetus from the discovery by Hippalus in AD 45 of the "monsoon winds flowing regularly across the Indian Ocean." Apparently this aided the prosperity of the north-western Deccan. Well-marked traces of a busy trade-route between Ter and Paithan and the west coast of India still remain, and in *The Periplus of the Erythraean Sea* a Greek navigator recorded in the first century that "ships built and fitted by the Indians sailed with their merchandise of pearls, precious stones, spices and fine cotton cloth called muslin."

The discovery of coins in the Deccan with heads of Roman Caesars and the head of the Buddha with the Imperial mask has left little doubt that "Andarae," recorded by Pliny, was connected with the classical world of Graeco-Roman art and that this influenced the dramatic episodes in the narrative technique of Buddhist art. Furthermore, overland trade exchanges with international centres such as Palmyra, Petra, Alexandria and so on, facilitated cultural intercourse, particularly when the message of Buddhism left India's confines to become a world religion. Greek, Christian, Zoroastrian and Central Asian influences infiltrated into Indian cultural centres such as Taxila and Mathura through works of art carried there by traders, pilgrims and craftsmen. The mixed Graeco-Romano-Indian culture at Gandhara produced images of the entire Buddhist pantheon. Craftsmen from Asia Minor such as Agesilas evolved a hybrid school of art in the Kushan court, in which the whole range of Imperial Roman imagery and Hellenic style were so transplanted that the Buddha appeared in the robes of an Athenian philosopher. Some of this influence percolated perforce to Ajanta through the patronage of the Saka princes, the western Satraps, who had considerable influence in Malwa, Kathiawar, Saurashtra and the Konkan from about the first century BC to the fourth century AD.

Nevertheless, the dominant aims at Ajanta, which were invariably aesthetic and devotional, remained undisturbed. The most fleeting as well as the most profound aspects of life continued to be expressed intensely through a linear rhythm of harmonious elements that belongs to Ajanta alone. The foreign elements incorporated at Ajanta, such as the drapery in Graeco-Roman style and the foreign characters in the Persian Embassy scene (Pl. 23), or the fur-trimmed conical caps and embroidered coats on the group of rulers listening to the First Sermon of the Buddha in Cave XVII, are sparse and very dissimilar to their prototypes. So are the Bacchanalian scenes painted in several places on the ceiling of Cave I and the quaint bearded figure with a pair of striped socks and a skull-cap, drinking wine with his boon companion, in the veranda of Cave II. These paintings with their obvious foreign influences do not in the least show the typical rigid features of a suburban art produced by virtuosos according to accepted conventions. They still retain the vitality of original models and the sincerity and devotion of the people. The Bacchanalian scenes of drinking and dancing are pervaded by the traditional Indian love of dancing which induces subtle, lyrical movements.

Long before Hellenistic painting reached Ajanta, it had stumbled and fallen as at Miran in Central Asia, where wall-paintings of the third century AD, depicting Buddhist scenes, have heavy contours, full faces and prominent eyes like the portraits found in Egyptian tombs, but quite unlike the elegant, refined, tender and animated types at Ajanta. In the process of stressing the spiritual, rejecting the superfluous and adapting the lucidity and dramatic power of formative art,

the Ajanta masters of the Mahayana period maintained an effective medium of their own. They did not adopt the monotonous reiteration of Persian motifs and ideas, the grotesque exaggeration of Syrian fancy or the spaciousness which is typical of Persian art, as these features obstructed the eloquent expression of their beliefs and their deep intuitive sympathy with nature.

"For, where pious persons, adorned with excellent virtues, have their residence, such a place is very suspicious and lovely, a sacred place of pilgrimage, a hermitage," says an inscription in Cave II. The beauty of rock-cut *viharas* or monasteries, and *chaityas* or places of worship, lay in the imitation of the nature rather than the appearance of things, and was determined by the coincidence in them of loveliness and utility. Of the five *chaitya*-Caves at Ajanta, IX, X, XIX, XXVI and XXIX, the last three belong to the Mahayana group. The *chaitya* bears some similarity to the early Christian basilica, having an arched roof and a long vaulted nave with pillared aisles on either side, terminating in an apse. In the apsidal end is placed the *chaitya* or *stupa*, which is in fact a sophisticated form of the grave mound of pre-Buddhist times. The façade, in the form of a screen with a small door, is usually surmounted by a prominent arched window to light the interior. The shape of this arched window gradually evolved from a simple semi-circular opening, as in the earliest *chaitya*-Cave X, to the elaborate sun windows of the *chaitya*-Caves IX, XIX and XXVI of a later period. Inside Cave X, traces of old wooden ceilings are still to be found, which the stone architecture of a later period faithfully imitated. With more experience and a greater degree of adaptation, the plain, leaning pillars of the caves decorated in the pre-Christian era gave way to upright, ornamented pillars in the Mahayana group of caves, just as the *stupa* dome changed from a plain hemisphere to a cylindrical form with elaborate carving and sculptures.

The *viharas* are rectangular halls with cells for the monks on the inner sides, leading out to verandas. The oldest *viharas* at Ajanta, Caves XXX, VIII, XII, and XIII, in that order, were the monasteries attached to the earliest Hinayana *chaityas*, Caves IX and X, which have many features in common such as a square central hall, without pillars to support the roof, opening into small living-rooms with stone beds, over which are the false berm-type windows. The *viharas* of the Mahayana group consist of Caves VI, VII, XI, XV, XVI, XVII, XVIII, XIX and XXVI, which are said to belong to the period between AD 450 and 550; of these, the last four have the same type of inscription and style of alphabet, whereas Caves I, II, III, IV, XXVII and XXIX were perhaps hollowed out at a later period. By the middle of the fifth century the plan of the *vihara* included the function of the *chaitya* by introducing imposing statues of the Buddha in place of the *stupas*. And in order to accommodate a more numerous laity an antechamber and a shrine in the back wall called the *chaitya mandiram* were added. The berm-type false windows were discarded, but the pillars, carved with greater zeal, surrounded the main hall and lined a narrow passage between the monks' cells on three sides of the hall. An inscription by Varahadeva, Harishena's minister, who dedicated Cave XVI, accurately describes the features of the new plan as well as the carved pillars, sculptures and decorations. The magnificent Caves I and II are both assigned to the sixth century (though the former is the earlier of the two), and represent Ajanta's resurgence of sophisticated painting in the face of the Hindu revival.

Curiously enough, most of the Ajanta paintings were created in the period of continued political upheaval and disturbed social conditions which followed the collapse of the Empire of Asoka, the Constantine of the Buddhist religion, when the new converts to Brahminism who ruled the divided successor kingdoms were often indifferent if not actively hostile to the Buddhist faith. The early Ajanta caves were built nearly a hundred years after Asoka's death. His extensive Empire, which at its zenith embraced almost the whole of non-Tamil India and a considerable part of Afghanistan, had disintegrated, and the flourishing world religion of Buddhism was on the decline in the Indian subcontinent. While in north-western India the Bactrian armies of Demetrius paved the way for the foundation of an independent Greek kingdom, which remained paramount in that part of the country for nearly a hundred years, in the Deccan a number of local provincial chiefs proclaimed themselves independent. Simultaneously with this development —perhaps as a reaction to all that the patron of the Buddhist religion stood for—most of the rulers of the divided successor-states disowned Asoka's state religion, and instead began to subscribe to the old Vedic rituals. Taranatha, the Tibetan historian, refers to a policy of religious persecution of the Buddhists by the Brahmin Sunga and Kanva dynasties of Magadha, which succeeded the

Plate 36

Shakti Pandara. Cave 1, second half of 6th century

Princess Irandati. *Vidhurapandita Jataka.* Cave II, end of 5th century

Plate 37

79

Plate 38

MOTHER AND CHILD BEFORE THE BUDDHA. Cave XVII, early 5th century

Maurya kings. From the middle of the first century BC to the beginning of the third century AD, when the Satavahana dynasty established itself in the north-western Deccan, the ascendancy of Brahminism among the ruling classes is recorded at Nanaghat, Nasik and Karle. The Satavahana king Satakarni II, whose empire covered roughly the modern state of Maharashtra, is noted for having performed sumptuous Vedic sacrifices. This precedent was followed by Gautamiputra Satakarni, who in addition introduced special laws in his dominion to "put a stop to the inter-mingling of the four classes" of the Hindu caste system which ran contrary to Buddhist belief.

Religious patronage apart, in the wake of the rising Satavahana or Andhra power in the first century AD, the monks soon found their abodes precariously perched on the frontiers between the dominions of the Satavahanas and those of their enemies in north-western India, the western Satraps. The passes leading out of the Deccan, along which the cave-temples were made, served as convenient outlets for the large-scale raids which were at that time India's conception of warfare. During the Saka-Satavahana duel, though Malwa was the main prize at stake and frequently changed hands, Nasik and the Ajanta chain of hills were also subject to fluctuating fortunes according to the political vicissitudes of the time. Paithan or Pratishthana, the Satavahana capital on the river Godavari, for some considerable time served as an advance military post to check the growing attacks of the Scythian invaders. In fact, some time after the death of Satakarni, the son of Simuka, founder of the dynasty, the Sakas of the Kardamaka family ousted the Satavahanas from the ports of the west coast and forced them to evacuate Paithan and to move eastward to Andhradesa, until Gautamiputra Satakarni (AD 62-86) appeared on the scene and "destroyed the Sakas." Paithan thus became the headquarters of his son Vasishtiputra Pulamavi (AD 86-114).

The sufferings of the populace as a result of this struggle are significantly recorded in Nasik cave inscriptions, in which Gautamiputra Satakarni is said to have "sympathized fully with the weal and woe of the citizens." But peace could not be maintained for long, and by AD 150 the Kardamaka ruler Chastana and his grandson Rudradaman twice defeated the Satavahana kings and recovered most of the northern and northwestern regions. The Satavahana kingdom survived for three hundred years or more, its power often reaching beyond the Narmada river into Malwa,

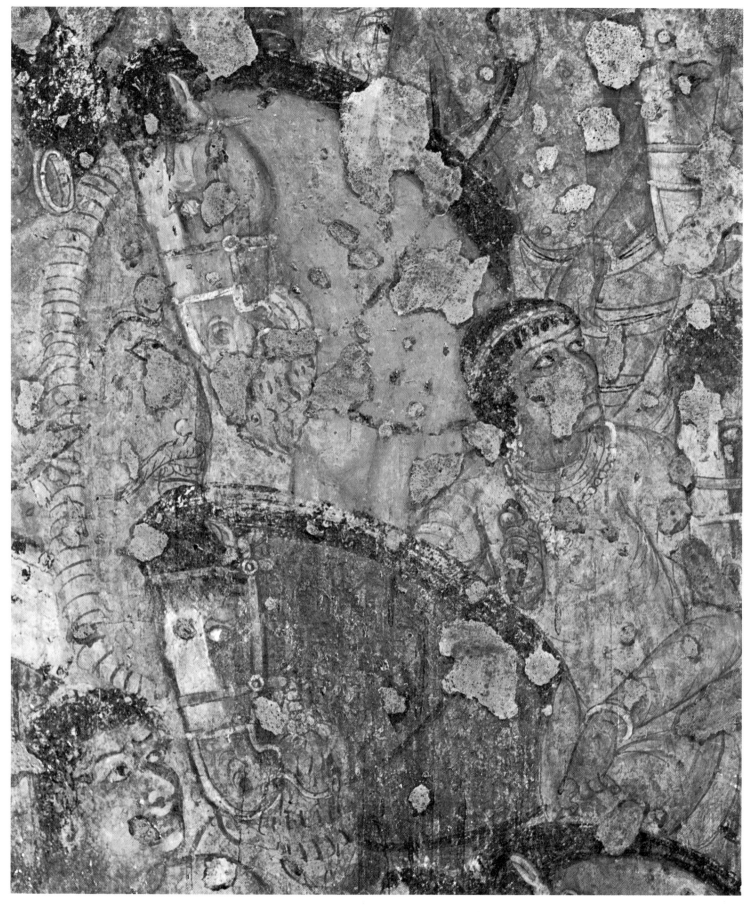

Plate 39

HORSES IN A PROCESSION. *Vidhurapandita Jataka.* Cave II, end of 5th century

and in the second century AD it extended from coast to coast before it disintegrated. Thereafter it is hard to visualize the prevalent conditions at Ajanta, as there was probably no government worthy of the name which could have been even remotely concerned with Bhogavardhana's security. The Ikshvakus enjoyed a short-lived sovereignty south of the river Krishna; the Chutu Satakarnis of Mysore were merely local chiefs; in the Konkan the Abhiras founded a principality but it soon sank into insignificance. The western Satraps, having been defeated by the Abhiras, declined rapidly during the second half of the third century. Nor in northern India was there any power capable of stepping into the place of the Kushan supremacy and bringing the Deccan under its hegemony.

Against this background of turmoil and uncertainty, the prestige and power of the common people seem to have been enhanced as they began to form organized groups (*sabhas*) and trade guilds (*srenis*) with prominent citizens as their representatives. The trend is recorded at Ajanta in numerous inscriptions such as those referring to the contribution by the lay worshipper Jasadeva in Cave IX, and "the meritorious gift of a dwelling with cells and hall by the merchant Ghanamadada" in Cave XII. But the "customs" or rules of the *sabha* made their weight felt, especially in the first half of the second century. Nasik and Junnar epigraphic records mention *srenis* of potters, makers of water-pumps, corn-chandlers, weavers, braziers and dealers in oil, and so on, which seem to have exercized considerable influence, especially when they began to receive cash deposits and endowments of property. A Govardhana weavers' guild, for example, accepted a permanent investment of a considerable sum of money, the interest from which was earmarked for supplying clothing to the monks during the rainy season. A corn-chandlers' guild provided a cave with cells. *Sabhas* and *srenis*, with their well-integrated social organization, thus became the community's main source of stability, expressing a common culture and a certain general view of man's nature and purpose.

This vigorous and self-conscious community life is reflected in a *Jataka* story which speaks of the villagers who "one day stood in the middle of the village to transact village business, and they (decided to) do good works; so they would get up betimes, and go out with knives, axes and

SUTASOMA JATAKA

Once the Bodhisattva was born as the son of Indraprastha's head wife and was named Sutasoma. He learned all the sciences from a teacher of world-wide fame at Takkasila, and in time ascended his father's throne. One of Sutasoma's fellow students during his stay at Takkasila was Prince Saudasa, who had been a yaksha in his previous incarnation. Saudasa was prone to evil ways and after he succeeded his father as King of Benares, he became a cannibal. His passion for human flesh became so acute that he secretly contrived with his cook to have his own subjects murdered. The people, with the assistance of the king's commander-in-chief, eventually discovered the man-eater and banished him from his kingdom. Saudasa then dwelt in a forest and having eaten his own cook, preyed upon all travellers who passed his way. On one occasion Saudasa was seriously injured. He lay down under a banyan tree and offered a prayer to the spirit of the tree saying, "My lady, nymph of the tree, if within seven days thou canst heal my wound, I shall bathe thy trunk with the blood from the throats of one hundred and one princes from all India." He recovered, and among others he seized Sutasoma when he was coming out of a lotus pool after taking a bath, and carried him away in captivity. Reconciled to his fate, Sutasoma asked the cannibal to let him go free for a day; he promised to return after hearing some holy verses from an ascetic and making an offering to the preacher of the law. Saudasa was greatly surprised by Sutasoma's good faith and courage when the Great Being returned the next day. Realizing what was amiss in his life Saudasa was converted from his evil ways by the gentle preachings of the Bodhisattva. From then onwards he gave up cannibalism and returned to the moral law.

VIDHURAPANDITA JATAKA

In Indraprastha, the capital of the Kuru Kingdom, there once ruled a raja named Dhananjaya. He had a minister called Vidhurapandita (the Bodhisattva) who fascinated all the kings of Jambudvipa by his wisdom and eloquence. On one occasion, the Naga King Varuna was so impressed by his speech that he presented Vidhurapandita with a precious jewelled necklace. Varuna's queen, Vimala, on hearing this, feigned illness and told her husband that she would die unless the minister's heart was brought to her. The perplexed Naga King took his most beautiful daughter, Irandati, into his confidence and entreated her to seek a brave husband who could fulfil her mother's wish. Irandati consented, and dressing herself in her finest clothes and ornaments she danced and sang on a bed of fragrant flowers as the Yaksha general Purnaka was riding past in heaven on his magic horse. He heard the lovely maiden's sweet song, fell in love with her, and subsequently promised to procure the heart of the Kuru minister. Purnaka knew of Dhananjaya's weakness for the game of dice, so he enticed the King to play with him by showing him a magnificent jewel with magical qualities. Purnaka thus won from him Vidhurapandita as a wager. On his way back to the Naga world, Purnaka failed in his many attempts to kill the minister. At last, to the Yaksha's utter astonishment, Vidhurapandita himself offered to tell him the way to obtain his heart. Purnaka was greatly touched and, admiring his courage and wisdom, brought him alive to the Naga Court. Varuna and his consort Vimala were equally enchanted by Vidhurapandita's wise words and after feasting him for six days in the Naga Kingdom, the Bodhisattva was allowed to return to the Kuru Kingdom.

Plate 40

THE GAME OF DICE. *Vidhurapandita Jataka.* Cave II, end of 5th century

crowbars. With their crowbars they rolled away the stones on the four highways; they constructed an embankment and dug tanks; they built a village hall; they showed charity and kept the Buddhist commandments." According to Buddhist canonical texts, a Buddhist *vihara* evolved on similar lines to become a self-sufficient colony, a kind of religious guild. This development inevitably brought about a healthy competition between various *viharas*, whose importance and legend largely depended on the value of their endowments and the resplendent imagery of their art forms. The result was an intense interplay of influences and ideas among creative artists and craftsmen, who now preferred to move from one *vihara* to another according to demand rather than be immobilized by assured status in the same monastery. The spread of Mahayana virtues over the subcontinent inspired and demanded aesthetic standards of high uniformity, in order to cater for the discerning tastes of the emergent upper middle class which supported the *viharas* with donations. In these circumstances, the main preoccupation of the Buddhist *viharas*, apart from the political vicissitudes of the time or the adverse religious affiliations of the rulers, was the everpresent possibility of the arbitrary withdrawal of support and patronage by the prosperous community.

Their concern was well-founded, because, in the wake of resurgent Hinduism, the romantic legend of Krishna, the hero of the *Mahabharata*, began to have a compelling appeal to the community's imagination and depleted the ranks of their own followers. The anecdotes narrating the amorous adventures of the cowherd-god, who teased and flirted with the lovely milkmaids of the Vrindavan forest, and his benevolent acts of chivalry and the tales of his unmatched bravery found a spontaneous response in millions of hearts. Therefore, to check the declining popularity of the Buddhist faith, the Ajanta caves, like other Buddhist shrines in India, were forced to become islands of philosophical and artistic resistance against the waves of the Krishna legends which rolled in from the forests of Karnool, the plains of Tamil Nad, the basin of Pennar and the foot-hills of Karnataka. As the Jesuits in midsixteenth-century Europe, faced with the growing influence of the Protestant Reformation, decided to enliven religious art in order to attract worshippers to the church, so the Buddhist monasteries seem to have found an answer to their problems in a

A Naga Chief. *Vidhurapandita Jataka.* Cave ii, end of 5th century

Plate 41

style of art which was impressive, sensuous, dynamic, emotive and even romantic. This was indeed an exciting development which facilitated the transition from archaic Buddhist art to the classical phase.

Unfortunately, at Ajanta there are hardly any examples of painting left to illustrate this evolution in terms of style. But there is a parallel to Ajanta painting in the magnificent second-century *stupas* built in the university town of Nagarjunakonda on the banks of the river Krishna, and also at Amaravati, less than a hundred and thirty kilometers downstream. Here, inspired not only by the Buddhist art of Bharhut and Sanchi but also guided by the lingering tradition of the ivory-workers of ancient Bhilsa, who created the tree spirits and genii, the cult of Krishna found new expression in the spaces on the long stone beams between the roundels depicting scenes from the life of the Buddha. The gaps are now occupied by pairs of lovers, the *mithuna* figures, in a delightful variety of poses and gestures. The "conversation pictures," as they are called, do not yet display the unabashed eroticism of tenth-century India. Whether it is the figure of a man gently placing his arm around his beloved's waist, entreatingly offering her a drink, or wooing her by tucking a flower in her hair, the miniature scenes never overstep the borders of propriety. Significantly, they are compositionally subordinated to the scenes depicting religious motifs. All these are seen at Ajanta, as for example in the eight panels painted above the entrance to Cave XVII. The evolution of this style is particularly noticeable at Amaravati in the gradual elongation of forms to make them look more suave and elegant. This is combined with the flexible curvature of human figures to infuse a greater degree of sensuality, and a larger variety of gesticulations to emphasize expression and emotion. The well-proportioned female figures and broad shouldered sturdy males of the *mithuna* figures are characteristic features of the artistic activity of this period. They are bursting with vitality and have a tendency to flow out of their frames. The teeming world of imagination in the painting of lovers and other secular persons with their feeling for the eternal beauty of youth and the joy of sensuality, which later reappears at Ajanta, support the supposition that at Ajanta, too, a parallel development was in full swing. Indeed, between the first and third centuries the art of painting enjoyed wide popularity, as is recorded in the *Kama Sutra* of Vatsyayana.

During this period, drawing panels, paints and brushes were among the normal paraphernalia of a gentleman, who was expected to know the six canons of drawing and painting :

Rūpa-bhedaḥ, pramanāni, bhāva-lavanya-yojanaṁ
sādṛśyaṁ, varnikā-bhanga iti citraṁ sadangakam.

"The differentiation of types, rules of proportion, the embodiment of sentiment and charm, the correspondence of formal and pictorial elements, the preparation or analysis of pigments, these are the six limbs of painting."

Thus the increasingly discriminating patronage of a large section of the community with practical knowledge of the art of painting can be said to have contributed as much towards aiding the transition from the archaic to the classical as the interaction between the *vihara* cultures and the restless competition among the artists. The middle-class patrons, while giving rationalistic support to the underlying conventional tendencies, seem to have exercized a continuous pull in the direction of naturalism. In terms of time, the formulation of this attitude coincided with the period of Satavahana sovereignty and the emergence of the Vakatakas, and in style with the general upsurge of Southern or Andhra artistic influences.

After the exquisite paintings in Caves IX and X, especially those depicting the *Syama* and *Shaddanta Jatakas* and *The Raja with his Retinue*, there followed a gap of several centuries. The lone exception perhaps is the animal frieze along the stylobate in Cave IX, which is considered by Hermann Goetz to have been done under the Mahakshatrapa's influence, somewhere in the late second or early third century. Its style is akin to Syrian frescoes of the Roman period or, more precisely, to the Miran frescoes in the Southern Tarim basin. As the motifs are not uncommon in Gandhara art or in Kushana sculptures from Mathura, the painting might well belong to another period. Even if Goetz is correct, the frieze is of little import, as it does not establish a link, as far as style is concerned, between the earliest and the classical phases of Ajanta art.

The end of the archaic and the blossoming of the classical period cannot be better represented than by the *Simhala Avadana* frieze. It is undoubtedly the boldest and the most grandiose composition in the history of Indian painting, a single composition of unparalleled power. Painted over an entire wall in Cave XVII, it is a remarkable historical record of India during the reign of the Vakatakas, and of the unabated hegemony of the middle-class patronage of Buddhist *viharas*. For Vindhyashakti, who was born of a middle-class family and who ushered in the Vakataka dynasty in about the year 255, appeared on the Ajanta scene more or less in the image of Simhala, to whose exploits this frieze of unmatched beauty is devoted. Simhala was the handsome and accomplished son of a merchant, who, after escaping from a shipwreck, vanquished hosts of ogresses and eventually colonized their island to become the king of Tamradvipa. Vindhyashakti was not regarded as a full-fledged monarch even by the Vakatakas and his name was omitted from the copper-plate genealogical records of the dynasty, whose family tree went back to Pravarasena. The eloquent inscriptions referring to Vindhyashakti, "whose strength increased in great battles, whose valour was irresistible even to the gods, and who was mighty in fighting and charity," are relevant to the episodes depicted in the painting. The shipwreck, his life of pleasure, his escape on the back of a big white horse, the pursuit by an ogress and her entry into the king's harem, the destruction of the king and finally the hero's victory due to his presence of mind and courage are all significant in terms of the spirit of the time.

In the midst of these scenes portraying battles and the turmoils of war, the panel at the same time marvellously recreates an atmosphere of pleasure in the beauties of nature by means of a very simple and natural style. The men are heroic and the women wear the simplest coiffures, with usually a plain ribbon and a few flowers tucked in the hair. Their ornaments generally consist of single strand pearl necklaces, plain round earrings and sometimes a ring. Their charming and delicate expressions do not yet have the affected behaviour and display which unfortunately became so much the vogue in late Ajanta pictures. Wigs were not known at the time although corkscrew curls were occasionally beginning to drop over the temples. The costumes are not intricate, and for that reason freely reveal the slender bodies. Both the men and women are mostly

94

represented as definite ethnic types, with a fair or reddish-brown complexion, which obviously points to northern influences.

In fact the advent of the Vakataka dynasty once again made it possible for the Ajanta inhabitants to renew their contacts with India's northern cultural centres. For a considerable time the hazardous conditions, already mentioned, along the northern wall of the Deccan tableland had discouraged such intercourse. Vindhyashakti's adventures were no more than isolated, nibbling raids on the bordering territories of the Satraps, but when his eminent son Pravarasena appeared on the scene, the Sakas suffered a serious blow. Having established his authority in northern Maharashtra and the western districts of Madhya Pradesh, the victorious Vakataka, taking advantage of a revolt in his enemy's kingdom, reduced the Satraps to feudatory status. The growing prestige and influence of the Vakatakas thus began to attract artists and craftsmen from distant centres in the north. By the middle of the fourth century, after the house of Vakataka had divided into two branches, the northern artistic influences were further strengthened as the main branch shifted its capital to Nandivardhana in the Nagpur region. The northern regions of the Nandivardhana branch bordered on the dominating Gupta Empire of north India, so that the main offshoot of the family came under the influence and patronage of the powerful Emperor Chandragupta II, who in 380 gave his daughter Prabhavatigupta in marriage to the Vakataka Rudrasena II. Prabhavatigupta's husband accepted the Vaishnavite faith of the Guptas and under their protective benevolence, if not their rule, the main branch of the family survived until the end of the fifth century. The alliance also seems to have secured the Guptas' southern flank in the successful military campaigns of 400 and 410 against the Sakas in the West. But by the time Harishena of the collateral branch rose to power in 475, the Vatsagulma or the Basim branch of the Vakatakas, reigning in southern Berar, had acquired the dimensions of a powerful state. It is said that at the time of Harishena's death in about 510, the power and prestige of the Vakataka Empire extended over practically the whole of the Deccan.

It was in the northern cultural centres such as Sarnath, Buddh Gaya, Taxila and Mathura, with which Ajanta thus came in contact, that the influence of the superb achievement of the

Plate 43

THE LOTUS IN THE WONDERFUL LAKE OF BRAHMADATTA. *Mahahamsa Jataka.* Cave II, end of 5th century

A Gate in King Brahmadatta's Palace. *Mahahamsa Jataka.* Cave ii, end of 5th century

Plate 44

97

Figure 7

Mathura craftsmen appears to have been greatest. The classical image of the Buddha was perfected at Mathura, though it is uncertain whether the Buddha's image was produced here for the first time or was invented by the Gandhara artisans working under the patronage of the Kushan princes and noblemen. In any event, it is generally accepted that, while the exquisite depiction of drapery reflected a Hellenistic origin, the surpassing beauty of quietism and kindliness in the facial expression of the Buddha image was a Mathura contribution. The craftsmen of Mathura surely had in the back of their minds not only the visual image of the "Great Person" as defined by the Pali texts but also the tradition of the colossal Yakshas of the later centuries BC.

These Mathura images, effectively portraying the ideal of the liberation of the spirit and the inner beauty of the saviour, became the epitome of that dignified restraint which is characteristic of the One who had set his heart on the goal of infinite understanding for all beings. The model was eagerly adapted by the major contemporary art schools of the Mahayana Buddhist world to fill the representational blank which was created by the cult of personal devotion in lieu of devotion to a code of ethics. The image came into being because it was needed in itself, and not because a need had been felt for "art." Therefore, in terms of style, it created new problems because the arrival of this new classical sobriety in an art which was already imbued with the vivaciousness and sensuality of beautiful females naturally provoked an apparent antithesis. The lovely women, originating in the nymphs and dryads, living a carefree life in the trees and the rivers of the pagan forests, appeared out of place when confronted with the formal conventions and precepts which created the Mathura Buddha.

The contradiction in style was especially marked because in the creation of the Buddha figure, the anthropomorphic imagery did not have the humanistic or naturalistic basis which led to the supremacy of figure over form in European art after the Middle Ages, or in Greek art after the sixth century BC. Here the attempt was primarily to portray an intelligible form or formula and not anything that had been physically seen. As is plainly enough set forth in Pali texts, "the form of humanity which had nothing to do with time" was clearly distinguishable from the portrayal of common mortals. The stylistic difference between the sacred and the secular subjects which is evident even at Mathura where the master-type was evolved, had a similar development at Ajanta. Yet the beginnings of the new style of drawing the sacred images, which was probably adapted by the monasteries some time in the second or third century, cannot be determined with certainty; nor do we have any surviving images of a period which could be compared with the earlier, rather clumsy Mathura models. Nonetheless, during the Vakataka period the disparity between the two styles can be observed, especially in the earliest existing Mahayana paintings. One particular example is the large panel, *Mother and Child before the Buddha* (Pl. 38). Between the portion depicting the colossal figure of the Buddha, and the area containing the two comparatively miniature figures of the woman and the child, there appears to be little consonance of either style or composition. The relationship depends mainly on the subject matter. Believed to represent Gautama's wife Yasodhara and their son Rahula, the two figures are restricted to the typical small-size Hinayana rectangular frieze, and are scarcely noticeable against the majesty of the Master, who is clearly inspired by the large-sized Mathura or Sarnath models.

Plate 45 A Buddhist Nun from The Great Miracle of Sravasti. Cave VI, middle of 5th century

THE BODHISATTVA. Cave IX, late 5th century

Plate 46

101

Figure 8

This anomaly of size is even more accentuated by the differing styles of drawing. The natural poise and movement of both the mother and the child, as they gracefully turn and lean forward to offer alms to the Buddha, show a highly developed manner of figure drawing and a thorough study and knowledge of the human body. It is a continuity of the Ajanta specialization, the beginning of which is to be found with incredible familiarity in the general attitudes and identical postures of the women approaching the Bodhi tree, seen in the painting *The Raja with his Retinue*. In contrast, the drawing of the Buddha figure still betrays the inadequacies which are inevitable in the experimental stages of transplanting a rigid iconography which had its roots in a different soil. The straight fall and rectangular form of the Buddha's robe, the crude drawing of the hands, and the absence of those flowing transparent garments falling on the smooth, beautifully moulded limbs of the classical Gupta period, testify to the new arrival of the image at Ajanta. Here, even if the Buddha's calm features convey the serenity of self-transcendence, the stiffness verging on monotony in the drawing of the rest of the figure has not yet been completely overcome. We have here, then, a phenomenon we might call a dual-style, consisting on the one hand of the large-sized, sober modelling of the Buddha and Bodhisattvas in which the sacred character was never belittled, and on the other of the decorative vivacity and evocative sensuality of secular subjects. This is most similar to the distinction between the Byzantine and the Roman artistic attitudes, one abstract and conceptual and the other concrete and perceptual. But when married together at Ajanta, the two halves of the dual-style succeeded in recreating a novel unity in diversity. It reflected the excitement and languor of a mixed feeling of the transient character of

THE QUEEN FAINTS AT THE SIGHT OF THE TUSKS. *Shaddanta Jataka.* Cave x, late 1st century BC

human existence among the cheerfully sensuous scenes of everyday life, and partly explains the paradox of the painting which, with its central theme of renunciation, of the extinction of desire, at the same time created some of the finest of all Asia's figure drawing, especially of the fair sex.

In this context, if we must tease ourselves with sources of styles and origins of concepts, the appelation "Gupta style," usually given to Ajanta painting, is literally a half-truth. The term refers to the northern Indian influences in a general sense, and more precisely to the drawing of the sacred images. For the rest, and this was the whole life of ancient India in panorama, there can be no better epithet than "Ajanta style." A few flowers strewn on the walls by other cultural centres already mentioned naturally imparted their colours and hues, but their peripheral effects were soon absorbed by the predominantly secular message of the monasteries. The world of the Ajanta princes in their palaces, royal processions with decorated elephants and horses, hunting scenes, loving couples, shopkeepers, porters with loads slung over their shoulders, ascetics in monasteries, peasants, beggars, and hosts of other people, surrounded by a fantastic variety of beasts and birds and flowers, were perpetuated by the trained hands of many craftsmen. The creation and interpretation of all this in masterfully drawn pictures on delicately painted walls is undoubtedly an indigenous contribution of Ajanta.

Above all, Ajanta's creative genius lies in the portrayal of women. The lovely ladies of the courts with their handmaids, the dancers and the musicians, the devotees, the common women and even the beggar girls are all drawn with brilliant zest and extraordinary knowledge. The conventions and orthodox attitudes which the painters adopted for their immortal, transcendental

Plate 47

THE DANCING GIRL WITH MUSICIANS. *Mahajanaka Jataka*. Cave 1, end of 6th century

archetypes, were deliberately set aside when they outlined the attractive mortals. The decorative, ornamental value of these lovely women was, as it were, too precious an asset to be subordinated to or diminished by the pictorial formulae for drawing the Buddhas and Bodhisattvas. Whether they are painted in repose, talking to their lovers, instructing their handmaids, admiring themselves in mirrors, carrying offerings, lifting the loads off their slaves' heads, or simply standing, sitting and gossiping, they are always painted with a sort of wonder akin to awe. Each time a woman is sketched, a feeling of new experience and excitement appears to have run through the artist's veins as he struggled to reproduce the soft roundness of her breasts, the curves of her hips, the turn of her head, the contortions of her body, the gestures of her hands, or the slanting glance of her eyes. Like fresh blossoms the women are invariably refreshing and fragrant. Whether they decorate the palaces as they sit in groups like garlands, crowd together in the street scenes, embellish the windows by their graceful presence, lightly fly through the air in the form of nymphs or are strewn like single flowers in the parlours of houses, they radiate that sheer joy and exuberance inherent in copying the female figure. Even when in the shape of ogresses they lure the sailors to their doom, the feminine aspect predominates; they never lose their dignity and nowhere are they besmirched or belittled. Just as the Buddhas and Bodhisattvas are the central theme in painting the sacred images, in the orbit of secular subjects the women are undoubtedly the focal point.

This attitude achieved its glorious culmination in the most beautiful paintings in Cave XVI, dedicated by the commoner Varahadeva. These, together with the *Simhala Avadana* frieze in Cave XVII and the two walls in the "Hariti Shrine" of Cave II, certainly represent the classical peak of Ajanta painting. The experience and maturity in the technique of drawing and colouring, and the incredible balance of composition observed in the paintings of the "Hariti Shrine," have been justly compared to Botticelli's *Primavera*. The elongation of the figures, which at Amaravati began to impart suavity and elegance, is completed at Ajanta with unmatched perfection. The curvature of the figures is supple, flexible and simple, yet not exaggerated, and there are none of those excessive gesticulations which are typical of the later period. The flower-strewn background with hills and swaying creepers and banana trees, the gentle rhythmical inclination of the women

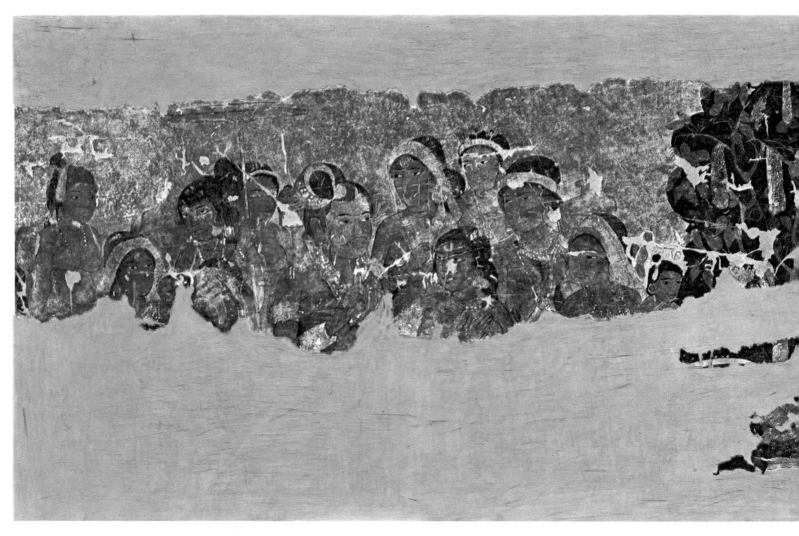

Plate 48

votaries with their graceful figures and gestures, the balanced distribution of the volumes over a large area, all contribute to the lyrical feeling of unsurpassed harmony and tranquillity. Comparing it with our standard Hinayana painting, *The Raja with his Retinue*, it is astonishing to find how a few elements of an evolving style, such as the elongation of the limbs drawn on an area with an enlarged range of vision, can so radically transform the pictorial atmosphere. The components forming the basic structure of these two paintings are almost identical. The figures of the women votaries in both the periods are drawn in a pose halfway between strict profile and complete frontality. The faces are similarly sketched, and in one or two cases the woman's head is elegantly turned towards her companion. There is a remarkable ease in the drawing of arms and hands; the arms bend at the elbows, mostly at right angles, or hang softly caressing the slightly curved hips. The exquisite, gently bending attitudes of the votaries as they walk along in the open air with uncovered breasts wearing simple attire and very few ornaments are also essentially similar in the

THE RAJA WITH HIS RETINUE. Cave x, late 2nd century or early 1st century B. C.

two processions. Yet the gentle and restrained votaries of the "Hariti Shrine" are no mere projection on a larger space of the care-free Hinayana devotees, but represent an entirely new concept of Ajanta colour and design. The remarkable illusion of warm reality achieved through unobtrusive modelling and calm linear harmony is reminiscent of Kalidasa's lyrical compliment to a young woman in his *Kumarasambhava*, "like a painting on which the final outline had been carefully drawn to mark the modelling of the limbs by the master painter Kamadeva." Kalidasa, the greatest of the poets and dramatists of India, is said to have visited Ajanta while associated with the court of Chandragupta II. He was one of the courtiers attached to the Vakataka court by the Emperor in order to assist the Queen Regent Prabhavatigupta in the task of administration after her husband's premature death in about 405. In his *Malavikagnimitra* the poet also speaks of the lack of correspondence between the beauty of the model and the beauty of the representation as *kanti-visamvadi* or "devoid of loveliness." This pointed the way to the transition

Figure 9   MAHA-UMAGGA JATAKA. Cave XVI, middle of 5th century

from the attitude of *paroksa-priya*, or "fond of the symbolic," to that of *pratyaksa-priya*, or "fond of the obvious." This is seen in the precise expression of emotion, the nervous linear elegance of eloquent hand gestures and the controlled turn and poise of the body in *The Renunciation of Nanda* (Pl. 53) in Cave XVI. There is as yet no picturesque prettiness when Sunderi, the beloved wife of Nanda, faints into the arms of her handmaids at the sight of her husband's abandoned crown, indicating renunciation. That stillness of unspoken sadness which can only be sensed at the moment of giving up all that is near and dear to human flesh is marvellously achieved. Sensual observation of everyday life, its involvement and simplicity, from delight in satirical fantasy and extravagances of courtly life to the extremes of mental pain and human indignation, are remarkably realized in this period. The artist seems to be delving into human and animal life with a kind of uncanny immediacy of response to the moment. In his depiction of suspicion, gaiety, the frown, derision, wonder, feminine insouciance, child-like innocence or thoughtful dignity, the artist's approach is governed by his deep emotions, poetic sensibility and fantastic imagination.

MAHA-UMAGGA JATAKA. Cave XVI, middle of 5th century   Figure 10

By the end of the fifth century, the classical upsurge of the Ajanta genius represented by the masterpieces in Caves VI, IX and X, and especially in XVI and XVII and the "Hariti Shrine" of Cave II, began to give way to what has been called Mannerism of Ajanta. In the language of style, it implied alterations in composition and also in figure drawing and decoration. The broad vision is progressively dissected into compartments so that the narrative is painted, not in an idyllic landscape, but in a maze of pillars of royal pavilions, palace windows, porches and balconies, city walls, shops and monasteries. Behind these brightly coloured pillars and other structures, a vast drama swiftly moves, in which the *dramatis personae* greatly outnumber their classical counterparts. The men and women start on their career of becoming more and more sophisticated, though they are not yet affected or effeminate. The men are still manly and the women feminine, and they wear simple clothes and few ornaments.

The early Mannerist approach is exhibited in the frieze *The Game of Dice* (Pl. 40), depicting the *Vidhurapandita Jataka*, which is painted on the wall of the right-hand corridor in Cave II. The compartmentalization on the right-hand side of the picture has not yet become a fetish, although

Plate 49   THE ROYAL KITCHEN OF KING SAUDASA. *Sutasoma Jataka*. Cave XVII, late 5th century

THE SUPERNATURAL CHILD MAHOSADHA. *Maha-Umagga Jataka*. Cave XVI, middle of 5th century

Plate 50

113

MAHA-UMAGGA JATAKA

This *Jataka* consists of a series of anecdotes about the Supernatural
Child Mahosadha and the four foolish sages, namely Senaka, Pukkusa,
Kavinda and Davinda, who were courtiers of the Mithila King Vedeha. The four, pretending to be very wise, became extremely envious
of the Bodhisattva, who invariably succeeded in solving the numerous
problems and riddles which were posed by the king to test their
intellect. *The Piece of Meat, The Cattle, The Necklace of Thread, The
Black Ball, The Sand, The Tank, The Boiled Rice* and *The Dog and The
Goat* are some of the well known parables. *The Son*, for instance, tells
of a certain woman whose son was grabbed by a female goblin. The
mother chased the ogress and seized hold of her, shouting "Whither
are you carrying my child?" The goblin replied, "Why do you touch
the child? He is mine." As they wrangled to possess the baby,
Mahosadha heard of the incident and sent for them. He asked the two
women whether they would abide by his decision. On their promising
to do so, he drew a line on the ground and laid the child across. He
then bade the goblin hold the child by the hands and the mother by
the feet. "Lay hold of it and pull," said the Bodhisattva, "the child
is hers who can pull it over." They both pulled; but as the child
cried with pain, the mother let the child go and stood weeping. The
sage then asked the crowd, "Is it the heart of the mother which is
tender towards the child or of the one who is not the mother?" They
answered, "The mother's heart." Thus the baby was restored to its
mother.

This *Jataka* also narrates the many attempts which the four wicked
courtiers made on Mahosadha's life. But they failed. The Bodhisattva,
having outwitted the villains in their many intrigues, finally triumphed
after numerous sieges.

NIGRODHAMIGA JATAKA

In a forest not far from Benares, there lived a number of herds of deer. At that time, the Bodhisattva was born as the leader of a group of five hundred deer and was called the King Banyan Deer. The Banyan herd was on friendly terms with another group which lived in the vicinity and was headed by the King Branch Deer. The animals were relentlessly harrassed by the King of Benares and his hunters because the monarch was passionately fond of hunting and he adored eating venison. The king's subjects were unhappy because their work suffered as they were obliged to take part in the royal hunt every day. The people therefore offered the king a park of his own where they undertook to cordon in sufficient deer from the forest for him to have his daily plate of venison without interfering with the routine of their lives. Their suggestion was accepted and in due course the park was ready; but when he noticed the golden skins of the two leaders who where among the first deer to be captured, the king forbade his cook to kill them. Meanwhile to avoid indiscriminate killing of their companions, the deer kings jointly decided to draw lots for the choice of the victim each day. This practice was followed until the lot unfortunately fell on a pregnant doe who pleaded for mercy. When no other deer came forward to help, the King Banyan Deer offered his own life as a substitute, and going to the place of slaughter, laid his head on the block. The cook recognized the golden deer to whom his master had granted immunity and informed the king of the incident. The king was so touched by the spirit of self-sacrifice and love for his subjects shown by the Bodhisattva that he proclaimed that henceforth no one should kill any animal in his kingdom.

Plate 51

THE ANXIOUS MAIDENS from THE RENUNCIATION OF NANDA. Cave XVI, early 5th century

Plate 52

Plate 53

the entire space is now overwhelmed with crowds of courtiers and ladies of the royal household. Unlike the classical method which achieved a relative balance between the major compositional volumes in a specific section, thus producing a feeling of calm co-ordination, *The Game of Dice* creates a sense of excitement and strain as the bodies are unequally held together in implied tension. Tension is also created by the tendency to animate many sections with a pervasive activity and this produces a feeling of overcrowding. This is evident in the depiction of the king and his courtiers when Purnaka displays the magnificent jewel to king Dhananjaya in order to induce him to play the game of dice. In the same frieze, however, the section on the extreme right showing *Vidhurapandita and Princess Vimala* at a palace window (Pl. 42) does not appear to be crowded. The calm linear harmony here is in direct contrast with the furore depicted in the part of the picture where the game of dice is being played. In other paintings of this period, the relieving calm and self-assurance radiating from the facial expressions of the Buddhas and Bodhisattvas were effectively brought into play so that within the framework of the dual-style the panels developed uniformly from calm, balanced proportions and expressions towards taut, nervous excitement, only to subside once again into the eternal bliss of the Buddhist *sunya*. The perfection in portraying facial expressions which the artists had already achieved during the ripe classical period was now further mastered. Yet slowly but steadily an element of sentimentality and romantic prettiness began to creep in. This is seen in the two finest examples of the Mannerist style of drawing women in Cave XVII, namely, *Sujata, the Farmer's Daughter* (Pl. 70) and *A Lady at the Court of Saudasa* (Pl. 71). The attractively poised maidens with a plain hair-style of simple buns resting loosely on their napes, matched by a few ornaments, arouse a feeling of innocent romanticism. The effect is enhanced as they elegantly tilt their heads and stare absent-mindedly beyond the noise and hubbub of the crowds that surround them. The women of Ajanta, as they step over the threshold of sixth-century painting, do not subscribe to Hinayana concepts of undiluted simplicity and unabashed naturalness, nor do they strictly adhere to the dignified restraint which characterized the classical manner. They strike a happy medium between the two. Nevertheless, the accomplished ladies of this transitional period were being unconsciously lured into the world-

Plate 54

THE BUDDHA AND THE ONE-EYED MONK. Cave x, late 5th century

A Yaksha and his Consort. Cave xvii, late 5th century

Plates 55 and 56

liness and exhibitionism of the Baroque style, even if they did not yet bend their bodies into exaggerated, serpentine contortions, refrained from twisting their limbs in superfluous gestures and cared little for glittering ornaments and spectacular hair-styles.

The introduction of Mannerism at Ajanta produced some of the finest examples of the sacred image, especially those of the Buddha, as dimensional disparities between the sacred and the secular were minimized and formulas of line-drawing and colouring were mutually exchanged. Apparently, there was only a brief period when the two facets of the dual-style, which continually underline the Mahayana painting, were beautifully balanced and pictorially on a par. As we have already seen, after the introduction of the Mathura image of the Buddha, the ups and downs of their respective achievements were often at variance. At the time when the creators of the "Hariti Shrine" votaries produced the two superb panels which represent the highest level of Ajanta accomplishment, the drawing technique of the Buddha figure was still trailing behind. But finally an equality between the two halves of the dual-style was definitely established with admirable effect, as shown by *The Buddha and the One-Eyed Monk* (Pl. 54). Here the Buddha, drawn in a reduced size, unlike the large, conventional and aloof Mathura Buddhas, is beautifully at ease as he sits half-turned towards the equally well-proportioned figure of the monk. The stylistic disparity epitomized by the colossal figure of the Buddha and the miniature drawings of the mother and child (Pl. 38) has given way to an almost uniform style of drawing the Master as well as the one-eyed disciple. Both figures have delicately drawn hands and well-placed feet, and are attired in identical flowing "Gandhara" robes; their countenances display those perfect facial expressions whose eloquence is matched only by the mortals of the classical period. The relaxed attitude of the Buddha, as he looks towards his overwhelmed, grateful devotee, is dignified yet unconventional, and the artist has succeeded in establishing an undeniable intimacy of spiritual unity and an unsurpassable pictorial balance.

The figure of the Buddha is perfect, but on closer examination, on the other hand, one will not fail to see the first signs of Mannerism in the drawing of the monk, such as the corkscrew curls and a hint of that typical effeminate curve of the hips. Obviously the technique of drawing the sacred image had not only caught up with the other half of the dual-style but had gained a lead over it. This stylistic advantage was achieved somewhat by default, since the restraint imposed by the conventions of the pattern-book and by precepts protected the artists from being completely overwhelmed by the vagaries and revelry of Baroque sophistication. In contrast, the secular half of the dual-style, because of its passion for the spectacular and the original, soon tied itself into knots of pearl strings and necklaces, and became involved in the bulging curves entwining the pillars and walls of the palaces, from which it was never able to disentangle itself. In the same cave, where the magnificent creation of the Bodhisattva Padmapani, with gentle, compassionate eyes and delicately formed lips, reigned supreme, there were also drawn the affected, grossly exaggerated attitudes of the characters who partake in the *Mahajanaka Jataka*. The eye-slits are stretched out of all proportion to the face, men look effeminate and women exaggeratedly feminine, with bulging curves and rounded breasts. Excessive ornament is worn by both men and women, and strings of jewellery hang from the pillars and pavilions of royal chambers. To sum up, affectation had crept in everywhere, and the style had begun to languish.

The Mahayana world of unrestrained, prolific imagination overflowed the narrow rectangular friezes of Hinayana painting, illuminating both horizontally and vertically the darkest nooks and corners of the caves. It produced a kaleidoscopic spectrum of integrated colourful shapes, which, as they gradually emerge out of the diffused light, acquire a steady, continuous clockwise movement along the path of the ritual circumambulation. The movement of the eye, coerced by the connected, serialized episodes, imparts a restless sensation of directed movement, and when the eye halts momentarily in order to impose a frame, the figures seem to be in movement themselves. The imaginary frame, as it regains its movement on the crest of the waves of swarming figures and objects, towards and away from the relief plane, seems to accelerate the cross-currents of motion. It floats in the beams of the mysterious light which illumine with varied intensities the painted surfaces in the multi-dimensional spaces of the pillared halls, antechambers and chapels. Between the spectator and the unfolding action of the painting there are no formal boundaries, corresponding, as it were, with the unbounded character of the congruity we find in nature. The problem of

Plate 57

A MAN WITH A DOG. *Mriga Jataka.* Cave XVII, middle of 5th century

122

One of the Raja's Attendants. *Vishvantara Jataka.* Cave XVII, middle of 5th century

Plate 58

123

Figure 11

THE CAPTURE OF THE SACRED
DEER.
Cave XVII, middle of 5th century

spatial representation and the means employed to indicate the movement or distribution of objects in space are approached in a way that optical plausibility of distances is different from the kind of perspective which is familiar to us. The distance in depth is hardly emphasized, and the figures and groups are well integrated with absolute simplicity in a sober background. This tends to be a narrow scene running parallel to the wall. Without being symmetrical, the whole is ingeniously balanced to create an interdependent harmony between successive scenes by deliberately discarding the frames and avoiding the diagonals in depth. In Laurence Binyon's words, "The more the frescoes are contemplated, the more does one appreciate the subtle relationship that connects the groups of the figures, so that though the unity of composition is not what impresses the eye at first, one comes in the end to recognize that a profound conception can dispense with the formulas of calculated surface arrangement and have its own occult way of knitting together forms in apparent diffusion." The dramatic intensity of all the components, integrated in an unlimited panorama of details, reveals the relation between life and natural things and the space in which they revolve, so that each individual part is indispensable and has little existence outside the whole.

Thus, in the transcending concept of an all-embracing life, is found not only the *leitmotiv* but also the inspiration of the painting, whose primary significance, as in any other branch of artistic activity at Ajanta, was ornamental. By virtue of its function as mural decoration and as an adjunct to sculpture and decorative carving, the painting at once seems to establish a congenial concord with the atmosphere of architectural cubism in the monasteries, produced by the vertical and horizontal flat surfaces of the walls in juxtaposition to empty space. The stylized projection of this unison is seen in the use of blocks of red, in the manner of the Ravenna mosaics, to denote the ridges of the hills in the "landscapes" of many painted surfaces. Here a strange symbolic magic, conjured up by geometrical virtuosity, is beautifully balanced with the "reality" of figure drawings. The shimmer of water flowing out in waves of parallel arches as in the frieze, *The Supernatural Child Mahosadha* (Pl. 50), is another interesting example. Similarly, trabeation, or the use of beams supported at either end by posts, being essentially in consonance with the vertical-horizontal

Plate 59   THE RAJA AND HIS GROOM LISTENING TO THE SACRED MONKEY. *Mahakapi Jataka.* Cave XVII, first half of 5th century

Figure 12

The Arrival of the Raja to punish the Monkeys.
Mahakapi Jataka. Cave XVII, first half of 5th century

127

MAHISHA JATAKA

Once upon a time, when Brahmadatta was the King of Benares, the Bodhisattva came to life as a big and strong Buffalo. He lived in the beautiful Himalayan regions where he roamed about freely in midst of the picturesque surroundings of hills, woods and caves. His favourite spot, however, was a large shady tree beside a brook of bubbling water. One day as the Buffalo stood resting under the tree, a wicked monkey saw him as he was sitting on a branch of the tree. The monkey could not resist the temptation of teasing the Buffalo, and jumped on his back. Then he disported himself by pulling the Buffalo's tail, slapping his back and began to swing from one of his horns. The Bodhisattva being virtuous, patient and merciful, suffered the monkey's misconduct in silence. Encouraged by the noble animal's tolerant attitude the monkey repeatedly played his pranks with impunity. A tree spirit who was watching the misbehaviour of the impertinent monkey asked the Bodhisattva: "My lord Buffalo, why do you patiently endure the rudeness of this selfish ape?" "Tree spirit," replied the Great Being, "If I cannot endure this monkey's ill-treatment without abusing his birth, lineage, and powers, how can my wish ever come to fulfilment? If he treats others as he now treats me they will certainly destroy him; then I shall be free and also delivered both from the pain and from the sense of guilt." Thereafter, to avoid meeting the monkey, the noble Buffalo left his favourite spot and went grazing elsewhere. After a few days another Buffalo, a savage beast, happened to see the lovely location which was earlier frequented by the Bodhisattva. He approached and stood under the tree on exactly the same spot. The wicked monkey mistaking him to be the Bodhisattva, at once jumped from the tree and started his old tricks by holding the Buffalo's horns. The fierce Buffalo immediately shook him off violently on the ground and before he could regain his senses the beast drove his horn into the monkey's heart, and trampled him to death.

SAMKHAPALA JATAKA

The Bodhisattva was once born as the son of the Magadha ruler in Benares and was named Duyyodhana. As he grew up and learnt all the princely arts, his father installed him in the Kingdom and unobtrusively retired to lead an ascetic's life on the bank of the river Kannapenna. There he lived a holy life in a hut, and developed the faculty of mystic meditation. Among the disciples who came to him regularly for instructions in the Law of the Buddha was the Naga King Samkhapala. Duyyodhana meanwhile had not seen his father for a few years, and he set out in search and finally discovered the hermitage, where he was greatly impressed by the overwhelming magnificence of the Naga King. Aspiring to be born as a Naga, Duyyodhana's wish came true, and at the end of his life he was re-born as Samkhapala. But soon he rebelled against the luxuries of the serpent world which were rapidly deteriorating his morals. Therefore, he decided to sacrifice himself by way of charity and with that in mind he lay on the top of an ant-hill. A party of sixteen hunters who were returning home saw the Naga and wounded him with their javelins. The Bodhisattva did not offer any resistance and said to himself, "today my desire will be fulfilled as I lie here. I will be firm in my resolution and yield myself up to them as a sacrifice." However, at this moment a land-owner named Alara, who dwelt in the city of Mithila in the Kingdom of Videha, happened to come that way and delivered the Bodhisattva from his persecutors in exchange for gold coins and precious ornaments. The Naga King then took his benefactor to his magnificient palace where for a whole year Alara was treated in luxuries and heavenly delights by three hundred Naga maidens. Eventually, influenced by the Bodhisattva's wisdom, Alara decided to renounce the mundane life and departed for the Himalayan regions to become an ascetic and preach the Law.

relationship of the cave interiors, appears to have suggested the structural perspective in the remarkable painting *A Monastery* (Pl. 30). The planimetric construction of a skeletal framework out of the alternately shaded bands of lintels and posts, as they proportionally recede in space to create an illusion of a third dimension, produces a pleasing pattern of rectangular and triangular planes and enhances the feeling of cubistic treatment. This style is also to be seen in all its sophistication of composition in *A Gate in King Brahmadatta's Palace* (Pl. 44), as masses of matter are refined and transformed into shapes, delighting us as we discover that they resemble bodies conceived geometrically. The sympathetic response of painting to rock-hewn architecture is further seen in the plasticity and solidity of human forms, animals, birds and foliage which dramatize and point the dynamic interplay of the solids and voids of the ribbed barrel-shaped vaults and sculptured pillars of the *chaityas*.

The predominance of frontal figures does not interfere with the plasticity of expression and the free movement, either represented or suggested—a tradition which was carried forward from the earliest times, at Mohenjo-Daro, in Maurya terracottas, and even at Bharhut. During the Vakataka period, a whole range of positions (*sthana*) was systematized from the frontal (*rjvagata*) to strict profile (*parsvagata*), just as a series of seven other distinct terms was specified to denote various degrees of bending and torsion of the body : *anrju* or back view, *sachikrtasarira* or a bent position in profile, *ardhavilochana* or the face in full profile but the body in three-quarter profile, *paravrtta* or head and one shoulder turned backwards, *prshthagata* or back view with upper half of the body partly visible in profile, *parivrtta* or the body sharply turned back from the waist upwards, and *samanata* or back view of a squatting position with bent body. The third dimension was clearly in mind as various positions were defined in terms of the distances from given points of the body to actually or supposedly suspended threads, and in terms of *ksaya-vrddhi* or "loss and gain," applied to foreshortening of the limbs, liberally used in a number of friezes at Ajanta. The relief and plasticity thus realized were further consolidated by the tones of the colours, expressed in Pali as *vattana*, or "shading," and *ujjotana*, or "adding high lights," and by the use of dark colours for the subjects in the foreground against a background of lighter shades, or vice versa. The three kinds of shading techniques mentioned in the *Vishnudharmottara*, namely *patraja* or shading like the lines of a leaf, *vinduja* or the dot and stipple method, and *airika* or stumping by means of a wash technique, are all observed at Ajanta to a greater or lesser degree. On the other hand, *ujjotana* did not refer to the lighter areas inevitably produced as a natural corollary to shading, but implied the method of specifically *adding* lighter and brighter pigments to produce an optic effect. While coloured areas always have clear outlines and the emphasis is invariably on the tactile or linear aspect of the composition, the optic style is frequently observed in different objects and figures, or in the panoramic effect in the same piece. The difference in feeling between tactile and optic treatment, which are distinguished in the *Lankavatara Sutra* by the terms *animnonnata* or "flat style," and *nimnonnata* or "high relief," is clearly indicated by comparing *A Lady of the Court* (Pl. 61) with *A Queen in a Palace Scene* (Pl. 17). In both cases the essential technique hinges on lines, but while in the latter the tones were added by partially concealing outlines and submerging details to produce an optic effect, the artist of the former, while aware of the possibility of composing tones, nevertheless created a strongly linear effect. Between the *nimnonnata* and *animnonnata* styles, the artists apparently enjoyed a wide latitude in employing the methods of line and tone, plane and recession, clearness and obscurity, balance and tension or rhythm and flow best suited to their individual talents and their subject matter. In the representation of the *Hamsa Jataka*, for instance, the pronouncedly static rigidity of the cubistic method of *A Gate in King Brahmadatta's Palace* (Pl. 44) is in marked contrast with the flat two-dimensional composition of *The Lotus in the Wonderful Lake of Brahmadatta* (Pl. 43), and especially distinct from the inner vitality and dynamic movement seen in the plastic expression of *The Fowler and the Golden Geese* (Pl. 65). In most cases, however, there is an amazing fusion of line, tone and plasticity.

Through a synthesis of the tonal suggestiveness of the light and darkness of monochromes, of *vattana* and *ujjotana*, the artists produced miraculous moods, as divergent and numerous as a woman's, by selectively drawing upon the experience and specialization accumulated through the centuries. But what is more amazing is the abrupt transformation of mood and expression brought about by a mere twist of line here or a deepening of a tone there. Within the sphere of the same

Plate 61

A LADY OF THE COURT. *Vishvantara Jataka*. Cave XVII, late 5th century

A Monk watching the Conversion of Nanda. Cave XVI, early 5th century

Plate 62

135

THE CONVERSION OF NANDA

After attaining enlightenment the Buddha visited his home town, Kapilavastu. His message of forebearance, compassion and purity of soul, refined by austerity, immediately converted his son, while his wife became one of the first of the newly founded order of Buddhist nuns. But Nanda, the Buddha's half-brother, being a weak character, was reluctant to join the order. The Master is said to have handed over his begging bowl to Nanda and asked him to carry it to the monastery. Overwhelmed by the monastic atmosphere and surrounded by other monks, Nanda agreed to have his head shaved and was thus ordained a monk. However, in the early days after his conversion, Nanda was never really happy with the monastic way of life. Once while the Buddha was away, he contrived to sneak out of his abode and made his way through the surrounding grove of trees. The all-knowing Buddha, as the legend has it, came flying through the air and alighted in front of the fugitive. Nanda quickly hid himself behind a tree, but as he did so, the tree was bodily raised into the air, exposing the unfortunate man to the Master's gaze; he was led back to the monastery. Nanda, discontented, still pined away for the love of his beautiful wife. The Buddha on hearing of his laments then flew with him to the Heavenly Suite of the Thirty-three Gods where Sakka, the king of gods, came to pay obeisance to the sage. Sakka was accompanied by five hundred pink-footed celestial nymphs who were far more beautiful than Nanda's wife. Fascinated by these beautiful women, Nanda decided to stay in the order so that he could gain this heaven in another existence. However, he was put to shame by the other disciples who ridiculed him for living a monk's life for the sake of his passions. Nanda, smitten with remorse, purified his soul and thus attained sainthood.

MAHAHAMSA JATAKA

The King of the Geese, Dhritarashtra (the Bodhisattva), was the leader of ninety thousand birds that dwelt on Lake Manasa. The commander of his army, Sumukha, was renowned for his wise guidance in matters of state policy. Now, it so happened that the King of Benares, Brahmadatta, having heard of Dhritarashtra's fame and that of his adviser, was seized with curiosity to meet them. He therefore constructed a beautiful artificial lake and proclaimed afar that birds who chose it for their abode could do so without let or hindrance. Dhritarashtra's tribe at first took no notice of the proclamation but when in the autumn a couple of geese saw for themselves the wonderful lake, they returned to Manasa at the beginning of the rainy season to tell their tale. They urged the Lord of the Geese to go to the marvellous place before the end of the rains. The Goose King consulted Sumukha, who advised him against the proposed journey as he said "The hearts of men are generally false and their compassion deceitful." However, the Bodhisattva, with implicit faith in mankind, reluctantly yielded to the wish of his subjects and, accompanied by Sumukha and his flock, set out for Benares on a bright autumn night. Meanwhile King Brahmadatta, anticipating their arrival, ordered one of his skilled fowlers to catch the golden birds. The fowler having laid his snares, the Goose King was caught; but unmindful of his own safety he uttered a special cry of warning enabling his flock to escape. Nevertheless Sumukha, notwithstanding the danger, stood by his master's side and even offered his own body as ransom to save his King's life. His noble words greatly touched even the hard-hearted fowler, who released the Bodhisattva and carried the two birds in freedom to the royal palace. The King was delighted and did them great honour, after which the Great Being and his faithful adviser preached the Law before returning to Lake Manasa.

Plate 63

A WOMAN IN A COURT SCENE. Cave XVII, late 5th century

Plate 64

139

medium, an antithesis between subject and character is evolved with incredible effect. Deep contrasts in tone appear to be generally equated with the grotesque banal facets of life, as shown in the facial expression of *One of Mara's Attendants* (Pl. 68). The serio-comic effect is principally created by placing the clumsy face in the shadow, accentuated by a few clownish spots of highlight on the chin, lower and upper lip, the nose and the two ungainly earrings. At the same time, the lighter areas compositionally balance the paleness of the skull and the band of the attendant's headgear. The result is one of ridicule, which at first gives the impression of being out of place, considering the abhorrence with which the Buddhist looks upon the Devil and his attendants, who attempted to deflect Gautama from practising austerity. Yet, the aptness of this approach can be understood if we bear in mind the compassionate and tolerant attitude of the faith towards other people's actions, and the subtle gentleness with which its tenets are propagated. In the Ajanta domain of art there are few pictures of torture or of horrifying terror. There is no sadistic realism or obscenity and there are no images that shout their meaning. The onlooker, therefore, instead of being summoned imperiously, is amiably led by delicate suggestion to distinguish voluntarily, and in a far more fundamental sense, between right and wrong.

In both the Hinayana and the Mahayana phases of development the illusion of volume is achieved by inflection of line and gradation of tone. But what is more noteworthy is the frequent intermingling, during the Mahayana period, of the *animnonnata* style of painting, where representation is achieved by simple juxtaposition of flat areas of contrasted colours in well-defined planes. This is explicitly seen in pieces such as *The Wailing Women* (Pl. 24). Hence, the often held assumption of a progressive evolution of style from the early plain, flat manner of the pre-Christian era, gradually "rising" to the *nimnonnata* style during the Mahayana period, is not convincingly substantiated. The two styles, as a number of paintings show, seem to overlap at every stage of the development of the art.

There are paintings from the earliest as well as the latest periods of Ajanta art which depict dance scenes. The dancers in the Hinayana frieze, *The Raja with his Retinue*, and what is possibly the latest Mahayana painting, *The Dancing Girl with Musicians* (Pl. 47), reflect a true standard of the state of society of their time, because in the olden days mastery in the art of dancing was invariably considered essential to personal perfection. The *Vishnudharmottara* introduces its chapter on painting with a discourse in which Markhandeya instructs King Vajra that without the knowledge of the science of dancing, the rules of painting can scarcely be understood. In another passage, the observation of nature and of the rules of dancing are indicated as the ultimate resources of the painter. Thus, a comparison between these two pictures gives us a fairly good indication not only of the appearance of the people and their social surroundings, but also of the evolution in the style of drawing and painting which took place in the intervening period.

The Hinayana painting, formulated in that atmosphere of uninhibited joy which was peculiar to the pagan world, admirably expresses the mood of the time in the naive, gay abandon of the girls with full, uncovered breasts and their carefree gestures as they merrily walk along with their two dancing companions. The groves in which the scene is enacted enhance the feeling of freedom. With their outstretched arms, their simple gestures and their obviously improvised movements, the two dancing girls do not in the least convey any suggestion of premeditated thought or action. They seem to have unexpectedly come out of the group to dance along the pathway, and perhaps take turns with others, until they reach their destination to worship at the *stupa*. The way in which every girl leans in the direction in which the group is moving produces a delightful rhythm which is somehow in harmony with the haphazard positions of the other figures in the picture. The scanty clothing and the few ornaments, such as bangles of conch-shell modelled on traditional folk ornaments (ancient specimens of which have been discovered near Ajanta, and in Paithan, Maski and Kondapur) indicate that there is no self-conscious bashfulness.

The spontaneous exhilaration depicted in the Hinayana piece is in notable contrast to the well-arranged, sophisticated dancing of the Mahayana period, in which the accomplished, professional dancing girl, fully conscious of herself, stands in the midst of her paraphernalia. Her rigorous training in the art of dancing is evident from the *tribhanga*, or the pose of the three bends, which she forms with graceful movement of the body, while her hands, without interrupting the easy flow of her arms, eloquently express the *mudras*, or ritual gestures. Her beautifully designed

Plate 65

THE FOWLER AND THE GOLDEN GEESE. *Hamsa Jataka.* Cave XVII, middle of 5th century

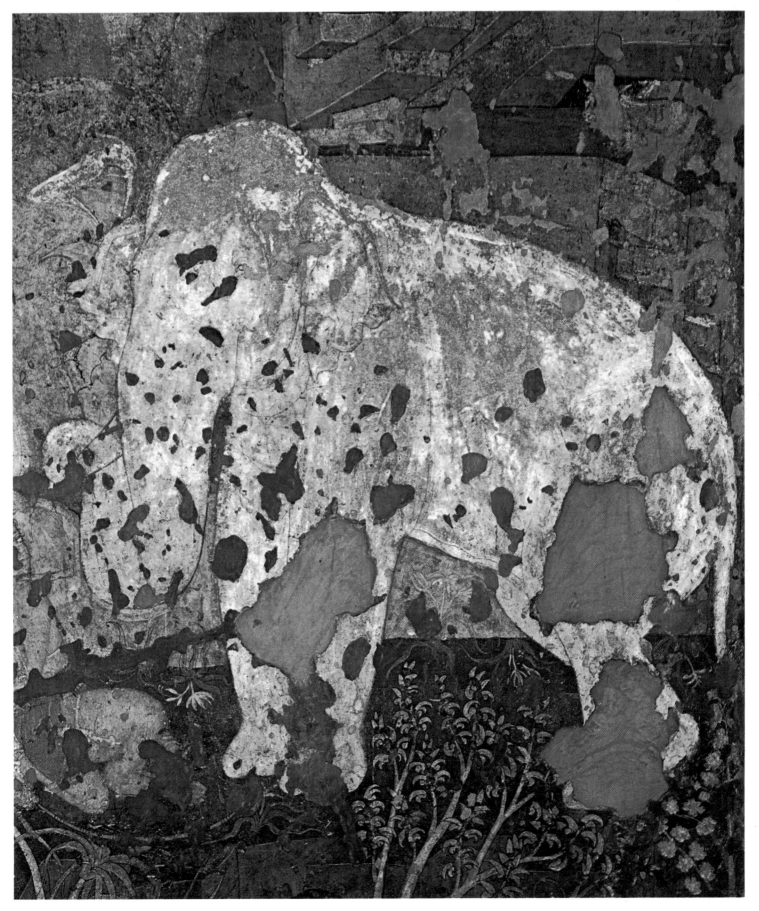

SHADDANTA IN A LOTUS LAKE. *Shaddanta Jataka.* Cave XVII, middle of 5th century

Plate 66

143

SHADDANTA JATAKA

Among the trees, lilies and blue, white and red lotuses of Lake Shaddanta, there once dwelt a herd of eighty thousand elephants in a golden cave. Their leader was a colossal white elephant (the Bodhisattva) who had two favourite wives named Chullasubhadda and Mahasubhadda. One day, when the herd had gone out to see the great *sal* grove in flower, the chief elephant unintentionally offended Chullasubhadda. In order to get her revenge, the vain wife prayed to be reborn as the Queen of Benares so that "then I shall be dear and near to the king, and in a position to do what I please. So I shall speak to the monarch and slay the elephant with a poisoned arrow." Her wish came true and, pretending to be sick, she told her husband that until the tusks of the white elephant were brought to her, she could not recover from her illness. Then she selected a cruel hunter, Sonuttara, and showed him the way to the golden cliff beyond which lived the elephants. Sonuttara dug a pit, concealed himself near the lake where the white elephant used to come after his bath and wounded him with a poisoned arrow. But when he failed in his several attempts to remove the elephant's colossal tusks, the Bodhisattva pulled them out with his trunk and gave them to the hunter saying "the tusks of omniscience are a hundred thousand times dearer to me than these are; may this meritorious act be to me the cause of attaining salvation." When the queen heard the story and saw the tusks, she could not endure the thought of one, who, in her former existence, had been her husband. She was overwhelmed with grief and died of a broken heart on that very day.

THE TEMPTATION OF THE BUDDHA

The Bodhisattva sat under the Bodhi tree in deep meditation in order to attain enlightenment when Mara, the Evil Spirit, approached him. Mara made many attempts to dislodge the Master from his resolve lest he should achieve the supreme moment and open up the path of salvation for mankind. Having scared away hosts of gods who were awaiting the great moment, the spirit of sensual pleasure and worldly passion at first tried to persuade the Bodhisattva to abandon his quest by tempting him with desire for power and glory. For days Gautama withstood temptations of all kinds. Having failed, Mara, disguised as a messenger falsely told the Buddha that his wicked cousin Deva-datta had rebelled, thrown his father into prison and seized his wife Yasodara. It was in vain. He then sent his three most beautiful daughters called Desire, Pleasure and Passion to disport themselves before the sage. They danced and sang and contrived every means of seduction; but the Bodhisattva rose above their wiles. Thereupon Mara summoned his demons and made a furious and appalling assault with whirlwind, tempest, flood and earthquake to dislodge Gautama. But Siddhartha, calm and unmoved, sat under the Bodhi tree. The frustrated Mara then challenged the Bodhisattva's right to sit on the spot and even demanded evidence of his goodness and benevolence. The Bodhisattva called upon the Earth to bear witness to his right by virtue of his acts in previous existences. This he did by touching the ground with his hand, and the Earth spoke with a voice of thunder : "I am his witness." Mara, defeated, fled in dismay; and it was in the course of the succeeding night that Siddhartha passed from the state of being a Bodhisattva to complete and perfect Buddhahood.

Plate 67

THE BODHISATTVA. Cave II, 5th century

One of Mara's Attendants from The Temptation of the Buddha. Cave 1, 5th century

Plate 68

147

garments, the variety of her glittering trinkets, and her bewildering coiffure admirably fulfil their intended purpose of making her the centre of attraction. This is also obvious from the expression on the faces of her devoted assistants and the voluptuous onlookers. Unlike the Hinayana painting, her sophisticated companions, who are as lavishly dressed, nevertheless seem aware of their subordinate status as they sit in two well-arranged groups, leaving room for the dancer to move about. The palatial surroundings and decorations, the accompaniment of musical instruments, the *mridangam* or drums, the flutes and the cymbals, the fantastic garments and elaborate ornaments have all successfully contributed to staging a spectacular scene; and yet that inner thrill of joy and fervour which *The Raja with his Retinue* conveys is conspicuously absent. Nevertheless, the graceful but affected movement of the Mahayana dancing girl has peculiar merits of drawing and colouring. While in both periods the tone and inflection of line give a full sense of volume, the perfection of technique in the later period displays an extraordinary breadth and confidence of draftmanship. The varying thickness of line is drawn with a free flowing sweep of the brush to depict the Aryan features of the oval faces, elongated eyes with arched eyebrows, aquiline noses, and fine sensitive lips. The lines have become darker to serve as a suitable accessory to the *vattana* and *ujjotana* techniques of shade and high light, which are added to accord neatly with the spirit and style of the period, tending towards exhibitionism.

The spectacular in painting, however, was greatly heightened with the exciting discovery of lapis lazuli, which was unknown at Ajanta until the fourth or fifth century. The artists now found in its cool transparent blue, which by its very nature appears to recede into the background, an effective medium for creating visual depth, within the limits of the Ajanta perspective, by contrasting it with the warmth of the red and brown tones, which seem to come forward towards the onlookers. The omnifarious blue colour infused a deepening of tonal vision by becoming a part of the structure of space and the intensity of light. The neutral tints of the chocolate-brown background of the earlier paintings are now frequently replaced by the offshoot of the blue, the blue-green, thus melting the chill of the pure colour into the soothing thaw of the natural deep green. The illusion of spaciousness is also evident at once in *The Dancing Girl with*

Musicians, where the reddish ochre, yellow ochre and dark brown tints applied to the dancing girl and her imposing costume stand out against a plain bluish-green background. Here the exciting new possibility of emphasizing distances by the use of colour is most ingeniously exploited by the sparing use of the precious blue in limited areas of the background, thereby pushing back the whole area of the landscape in direct relation to the depth of the colour. The figures of the Hinayana painting in Cave x are painted in brownish red or other similar colours as red ochre or shades of burnt sienna; but here the neutral background has failed to indicate the same perspective.

This new colouring technique is employed during the Mahayana period with considerable effect in a number of paintings to produce a sense of distance and depth, and thereby to enhance the feeling of movement and animation. For example, in a very attractive piece, *Monks in a Monastery* (Pl. 12), notwithstanding the *animnonnata* style of drawing, the artist has most successfully infused a feeling of animation into the discussion by painting the background bluish-green. In another context, the use of blue to represent the solidity and strength of swords and horns was perhaps inevitable, and it was so employed in a number of pictures. But the ingenuity of its use as a secondary medium to produce the effect of lustre or "pictorial shine" by applying it as a complement to the flesh tints of brick red, pale green and light brown, is a landmark in Ajanta colour application. For example, light is reflected on the non-blue areas by drawing blue lines below the eyes and this indicates not only the shade but also the brilliance *in the eyes*. The method is most effectively used in Cave xvii. It seems to have been extended to Cave i, where a miraculous variation is achieved in *A Dancing Girl in a Palace Scene* (Pl. 21). The incredible shine of silky softness infused into the blue of the dancer's jacket enters into the vibrant and graceful movement of her right shoulder and tilted head by means of a glittering light effect.

The drama and realism of the Baroque, or the spirit of the Mannerist approach which is said to distinguish the later phase of painting from the works of the pre-Christian era at Ajanta, seem to have been heightened through the introduction of the luminosity referred to as *chayatapa*, or "shade and shine." A kind of soft, modified form of chiaroscuro, this technique succeeded in casting that unreal, mystical light which makes the sacred countenances of the Buddhas and

Bodhisattvas radiate with a mysterious glow. *Chayatapa* is clearly at variance with the *vattana* and *ujjotana* techniques which delineated perceptual objects in order to obtain plasticity, but did not produce the pictorial representation of light.

The perfection of the *chayatapa* technique, supplemented by the cumulative luminosity and perspective achieved through the varied application of blue, is ideally exhibited in the calm plastic harmony of that *chef-d'œuvre* of Indian art, the *Bodhisattva Padmapani* (Pl. 25). The illusion of ethereal light gently thrown on the Bodhisattva from his left produces a soft shadow on the right side of the face and neck; but unlike normal chiaroscuro, the left side of the face is also treated with a deeper brown tone than the softly highlighted right cheek and nose. In conformity with the Ajanta tradition, there are no cast shadows. These are scrupulously shunned by the artists who realized, as did Leonardo da Vinci in his time, that direct light and cast shadows destroy the representation of true relief or volume. The luminosity is further enhanced by the masterly handling of blue, sparingly employed on the necklace beads and delicately applied on the fringes of the fresh lotus. This is reflected in the warmth of the golden brown and pearl grey of the Bodhisattva's complexion. At the same time, perspective is created in the background by the relative depth in space of the blue jacket of the woman behind the Padmapani's left arm, and of the blue birds in the conventional bands of hills in the top left-hand corner of the picture. The blue areas in the background are at the same time in dynamic equilibrium with the blues of the necklace and the lotus. The introduction of blue did not give rise to a new school of painting, but in the "blue period," as it were, the artists obviously became more aware of the unlimited possibilities of colour combination and its fascinating effect on form and space.

As we have seen, the two manners of the dual-style acquired a new admixture of mutual harmony, and in many cases even merged to become indistinguishable one from the other. The permutations and combinations, aided by the use of lapis lazuli, produced enormous variations in style. On account of this, the paintings have been compared with the works of various Italian masters of the Renaissance; *Bodhisattva Padmapani* (Cave I) has been compared with the paintings of Michaelangelo, Correggio and Bernini; *Mother and Child before the Buddha* (Cave XVI) with the

Madonnas of Giovanni Bellini; *An Apsaras* (Cave xvii) with Simone Martini's Madonnas; the scantily clad *Mithuna* figures with the nudes of the *quattrocento* artists Pollaiuolo and Signorelli, and so on. It is also possible that the diversity of mood corresponded to the varied sources of inspiration and regional preferences, as well as the individual temperaments of an up-and-coming group of young artists, who perhaps were commissioned on a temporary basis to do piece-work. This group was apparently quite different from the innately calmer, more traditionally-minded artists who normally devoted all their life to working and painting in the same *vihara*.

The presence of a new circle of artists, as a result of a pressing demand for more workers, seems most likely if we accept the hypothesis, recently advanced by Walter Spink of Michigan University, that the caves of the Mahayana period were hewn out within a period of not more than fifty years. This view, as far as it concerns the paintings, is obviously conjectural because of the lack of relevant data and the anonymity of the artists. Nevertheless, as brief periods of intense artistic creativity resulting in some of the greatest masterpieces have not been uncommon in the history of art, the probability of an analogous creative fervour at Ajanta, compressed within the period AD 450 to 500 cannot be disregarded.

The unrestrained colours in many pieces, which contrast strongly with the sober gestures of piety of the "traditionalists," reflect the ambivalent frame of mind of the ebullient newcomers. In the excitement of the possibilities created by the ascendancy of colour over line, they seem to have attempted a synthesis of established principles and their own manner. What inner necessity or symbolic values led each one to choose certain colours as a basis of harmony and composition is not easy to tell. Here was perhaps the beginning of an ever closer relationship between colour, mood and time, which reached its culmination in the Ragmala pictures, where season, hour, emotion and music become fused in colourful design and represented as painting. According to the *Natya Sastra*, each *rasa*, or emotion, had to be painted in its expressive colour : the erotic was dark blue; the merry and exciting was white; the pathetic was expressed in grey; the furious in red; the heroic in yellowish white; the fearful in black; and the supernatural or amazing in yellow.

Plate 70

Sujata, the Farmer's Daughter. Cave XVII, late 5th century

A Lady at the Court of Saudasa. *Sutasoma Jataka.* Cave XVII, late 5th century

Plate 71

155

Figure 13

The representation of a wide range of temperament and emotion in painting was evidently a post-Ajanta development in Indian aesthetics. Yet, if the sensuous exuberance of the splashes of brilliant red of *One of the Raja's Attendants* (Pl. 58) is placed side by side with the remorseful calm of the dull greenish-blue of one of the finest studies in expression, *A Lady at the Court of Saudasa* (Pl. 71), again one finds a link between the characterization of moods and the colour of the artist's pallette. However, it is possible that some of the pictures are actual representation of skin colours because in ancient India lime white and red arsenic were used as cosmetics for the face and limbs. The popularity of this is evident from the prohibition against the fashion in the *Vinaya*: "Monks, nuns, should not smear their faces, should not paint their bodies and faces." In any event, the singular fetish in this period of the uninhibited use of colour—reds, yellows, greens, blues and greys—to represent the complexion of the skin, does not indicate any discrimination against caste or class. Such an interpretation is clearly ruled out by a comparison of the green tone used to colour the soldier's skin in *An Army on the March* (Pl. 72), with the green complexion of the princess in the *Mithuna Figures* (Pl. 27).

In many other paintings as well, the varicoloured skin of the commoners is similar to regal complexions. The complexion of the most enchanting of all the women at Ajanta, *Shakti Pandara* (Pl. 36), popularly known as The Dark Princess, leaves little doubt that the newcomers, obviously disregarding any social discrimination, had usurped the right to choose and apply colours according to their own caprice, if not according to the mood of their models. It is also possible that they arranged their colours for the sole purpose of pleasing the eye, with the

result that the sunny, spring-like hues of the classical images were replaced by the autumnal brilliance of the Baroque. While the fundamental qualities such as learning (*pandita*), piety (*bhakta*), sensibility (*rasika*), and knowledge of technique (*acharya*) were retained, the colour was no longer regarded as a mere adjunct to the drawing. In the hands of the visionary artists it became an autonomous instrument with which to describe "the beyond." The new approach is reminiscent of Bhasa's *Dutavakya*, in which Duryodhana, after a detailed description of a picture, exclaims : "O what richness of colour (*varnadhyata*)! What skilful application of brushwork (*yuktalekhata*)! How explicit the painting (*suvyaktam alikhito*)! I am pleased!"

The creative period of Ajanta splendour and brilliance ended as mysteriously as it had begun. Some of the unfinished caves, which were quite obviously abandoned unexpectedly, show that the emigration took place over a comparatively short span of time. Even if some of the caves continued to be lived in for a few hundred years after the fifth century, the merchant wealth which financed the decoration and ornamentation of the shrines had apparently been exhausted. In any event, the administrators of the monastic establishment could not have foreseen the impending misfortunes and privations, or they would not have planned new *viharas* in the hard rock, only to leave them incomplete. The problem is an important one because, in the absence of other data, its solution might provide a clue to the dating of the post-fifth-century painting.

The chronology of Ajanta has so far been based on the unreliable basis of a few inscriptions, and on a comparison of the architectural forms in the caves with those of other monuments belonging to definite periods. For example, the rather crude paintings of the latest period at

Plate 72

AN ARMY ON THE MARCH. *Sutasoma Jataka.* Cave XVII, late 5th century

A Horse. *Mahakapi Jataka*. Cave XVII, 5th century

Plate 73

MAHAKAPI JATAKA

Once the Bodhisattva was born as The Great Monkey and lived in the Himalayas with a retinue of eighty thousand monkeys. Near the bank of the river Ganges there was a large mango tree whose sweet fruit the monkeys enjoyed eating. They were however cautioned by The Great Monkey not to drop any of the mangoes into the water. Not withstanding this warning, one large, ripe fruit did fall into the river and was accidentally caught in a fisherman's net. The fisherman, having never seen the like of it before, presented the mango to the King of Benares. Pleased with the exceptional flavour of the fruit, the King made enquiries and then sailed up the river with his army in search of the tree. At last the place was discovered and the entourage camped for the night under the tree. At midnight, as the herd of monkeys approached to eat the mangoes, the King ordered his archers to surround the animals and shoot them. The Great Monkey comforted his companions and said : "Do not fear, I shall give you life." He then cut out a bamboo shoot to serve as an escape bridge. Unfortunately, the shoot was not long enough and therefore to complete the bridge, the Bodhisattva stretched himself across the end of the shoot and thus let his retinue safely pass over his body. But Devadatta (the Buddha's wicked cousin) who was then born as a monkey, hurt the Bodhisattva, who fell to the ground with fatal injuries. Touched by what he had seen, the King dressed the wounds of the Great Monkey, but in vain, as the Bodhisattva having taught the Law of the Buddha, died, and thus obtained salvation.

MATRIPOSHAKA JATAKA

Once upon a time, when Brahmadatta reigned in Benares, the Bodhisattva was born as a magnificent white elephant. He lived with his mother in the beautiful dense forest of the Himalayan region. But he was not happy because his mother was blind, and the other elephants were unkind to her; they teased her and even prevented the white elephant from giving her the sweet fodder he brought from the forest. So he led her away to Mount Chandorana where, for some time, they lived in peace. One day the white elephant came across a forester who had lost his way in the forest for seven days. The man appealed for help and the Bodhisattva gave him water with his trunk and carried him out of the forest on his back. Now it so happened that at that time the king's state elephant died and a reward was offered in a royal proclamation for another fit for the king's riding. The ungrateful man betrayed the kind elephant by telling the king's hunters about him. Thus the Bodhisattva was caught in the lotus lake and decked with festoons and garlands, he was taken to the king's stable. The king was pleased with the majestic white elephant and offered him all manner of fine food; yet he refused to eat and said "without my mother I will eat nothing." The story quickly spread throughout the kingdom and people from all walks of life petitioned the king to release the elephant lest he should die. Overcome with compassion, the king finally gave him his freedom. Thus the Bodhisattva went back to his mother and when he sprinkled water over her from a clear pool, she was delighted to know of his return.

Plate 74

A BHIKSHU WITH A LOTUS. Cave VI, middle of 5th century

THE OGRESSES. *Simhala Avadana*. Cave XVII, early 5th century

Plate 75

Ajanta have been linked with the late Bagh paintings, the seventh-century paintings at Sittanavasal in former Pudukkotai (early Pallava period), the eighth-century Kailasa frescoes at Ellura (Rashtrakuta Dynasty), and even with the seventh to ninth-century wall-paintings of Chinese Turkistan. Early scholars, such as Fergusson and Ananda K. Coomaraswamy, connected them with the Chalukya school under the patronage of Pulakesin II (610-642), who was a contemporary of the Emperor Harsha and of the Chinese pilgrim Huang T'sang. In support of this thesis it has been suggested that the so-called *Persian Embassy* painting refers to a visit by Pulakesin in 625; other Persian genre scenes have been linked with the Sassanid ruler, Khosru II. The contention has been challenged by others who feel, with Le Coq, that the Ambassadors represented in this painting are not Sassanid Persians but merely barbarians from one of the East Iranian tribes who were then battering against the political frontiers of the Gupta Empire. It is therefore suggested that *The Persian Embassy* was probably painted at least a century earlier, and that the monastic organization disintegrated in the second half of the sixth century, when the west and centre of the peninsula came under the control of the Chaluka Dynasty. Pulakesin II swept across Maharashtra at the end of the sixth century, making Nasik his military capital, and is said to have worked against the Buddhist Councils of Harsha with a view to supporting the Hindu revival. Eventually the Chalukyas defeated the previously invincible armies of Harsha on the banks of the river Narbada. Harsha's influence was stopped from extending south of the river by the Saivite Pulakesin, and this is thought to have shattered any hopes the Ajanta monks might have cherished from the last splutter of the Buddhist torch, which Harsha attempted in vain to uphold. There is certainly an element of truth in all this. Yet, not only the Chalukyas and the Rashtrakutas, but all the important dynasties who had anything to do with Ajanta, such as the Satavahanas and the Vakatakas, professed adherence to the Brahminical faith, and at the same time Buddhism still enjoyed a substantial following among the people. Huang T'sang, the famous Buddhist pilgrim who visited Maharashtra about 630, records that there were over a hundred Buddhist *viharas* there and an equal number in Karnataka, in which lived some six thousand monks. He also states that there were over ten thousand people who subscribed to the Buddhist religion.

Thus the causes of the collapse of Ajanta have not been clearly determined. The reasons might well be the very same social and economic conditions which gave birth and life to its glorious tradition. As far as the Ajanta shrines are concerned, the heart of this social and economic system was Paithan. This important mart, barely a hundred kilometers from the monasteries, was frequented by rich merchants who carried on a brisk trade that fed the ports of the west coast. Ptolemy's geographical account and the evidence of *The Periplus of the Erythraean Sea* indicate that during the early centuries these ports had developed into flourishing commercial centres and were known by the Pali names of Bharukachha, Surattha and the famous Supparaka (present-day Sopara). These, together with Kalyan and Thana, were indispensable links in the chain of trade centres which prospered in the hinterland and on the Paithan - west coast highway. The steady flow of gold into India, which eventually made the Gupta period of Indian history literally the "Golden Age," was undoubtedly the result of India's ever-increasing commercial activities with the West in the first centuries of the Christian era. The most dynamic period, however, was from about the middle of the first century to the end of the fifth century. After the break-up of the Roman Empire in 475, trade began to fall off, as is indicated by the scarcity and degeneration of the coinage after 500, compared with the earlier Imperial Gupta period. Then trade began to be carried out again in fits and starts, but was mainly conducted with the Arab countries, as is revealed by references to the Tajiks (Arab Muslims and Iranians) in the Chalukya and Rashtrakuta inscriptions.

The changes in the overseas trade routes were paralleled by a deflection of the inland commercial arteries as well, especially after the Chalukyas shifted their capital from Nasik to Vatapi (modern Badami). While Ajanta lay on the direct continuation of the road running from the sea-ports of the west coast through Nasik, the routes from the royal capital of Vatapi in Mysore naturally did not utilize the Ajanta Pass. The diversion of the trade route, like the changing course of a river, left the Ajanta monasteries isolated and helpless, while in the Chalukya capital the stupendous figures and the grand sculptures of the Saiva temples were being created, fed by the surplus riches flowing along the new route. This was bad enough for Ajanta, but the catastrophe was made complete when another patron of Hinduism, Narasimhavarman (625-645), whose

Plate 76   THE FREED ELEPHANT MEETS HIS BLIND MOTHER. *Matriposhaka Jataka.* Cave XVII, 5th century

THE DEER HUNT. *Sutasoma Jataka*. Cave XVII, late 5th century

Plate 77

father had grabbed the hegemony of the Eastern Deccan from the Andhras, eventually defeated Pulakesin II and killed him in battle. When Narasimhavarman built the city of Mammalapuram on the east coast near Madras, the trade of Southern India began to flow east instead of west. In this way a continued period of financial stringency in the region around the caves depleted and finally terminated the donations emanating from the agricultural households, lay worshippers and officials of the ruling monarchs. Thus the lively culture of the first five centuries, sustained by the benevolent merchants in transit through Paithan, supported by the local *sabhas* and *srenis*, and stimulated by cultural intercourse with other countries, died down and was eventually stifled.

The light, however, did not fade before the prophetic and apocalyptic spirit of Ajanta, emerging from the unbounded Buddhist love and compassion for all sentient beings, was carried to the point of dream-like ecstasy as it crossed India's frontiers. Riding on the far-flung waves of Buddhism, the decorative and iconographic prototypes of Ajanta inspired the Buddhist art of the late Wei and the T'ang dynasties at Khotan and Turfan in China, the earliest landscape and flower painting of Champa, Cambodia, Korea and Japan, and also the frescoes at Sigiriya in Ceylon. The Ajanta manner of painting, as it travelled through Western Asia on its way to China, also imparted its technique and its classical style of subtle sensuality and ease of line to the Bodhisattvas and Taras of the seventh-century sanctuary of Fondukistan, and gave its linear elegance to the painted niches at Bamiyan. Inevitably, however, in the process of interaction and fusion with the conventional local Afghan and Persian schools, much of the finesse of Ajanta lyricism became submerged beneath the heavy outlines of darker colours. The only exception to this tendency toward heavy contours in bands of deeper pigments, is perhaps to be found in the wall-paintings of Tun Huang in Western China. Here, due to the close religious and political relationship between the T'ang Empire and India at the time, the softness of the classical Ajanta line appears to have been imitated with greater fidelity and zeal. The Muslim conquest, followed by the destruction of many important shrines, has unfortunately left us with only a few meagre specimens. But frequent mention in the annals of Chinese painting of artists who were reputed to have painted in the Indian style leaves little doubt of the widespread popularity of the Ajanta technique and design.

DESCRIPTION OF CAVES
AND
NOTES ON PLATES

CAVE ONE

One of the finest *viharas* among the rock-hewn temples of India, this cave has been dated to the end of the fifth century on the evidence of its architecture and sculptures. The monastery has the usual plan, with a veranda, a great congregation hall and a shrine. The veranda, with a cell at each end, is 19.5 meters long, 2.8 meters wide and 4.1 meters high. A central door with carved jambs and entablature leads into the main hall, which is 19.5 meters square. The ceiling is supported by twenty exquisitely carved and beautifully painted pillars, which are surrounded by an aisle 2.9 meters wide. Facing the entrance, in the rear of the hall, there is an antechamber, 2.7 meters by 8.3 meters, leading into the shrine, which is 6 meters square. The *vihara* has fourteen cells, four each in the right, left and rear aisles and two in the front. The façade of the *vihara* has been marred by the destruction of the porch, but it still contains several bands of fine carvings. Among these are scenes of the life of the Buddha, elephant fights and hunting expeditions. The columns of the veranda and hall are also profusely carved. The shafts have vertical and spiral fluting encircled by bands of lovely tracery. The bases of the capitals are generally ornamented with mythical animals, religious stories and a great variety of floral designs.

Large areas of the walls and the ceiling, once all covered with paintings, are much damaged; the surviving pieces of importance, in the order of Buddhist perambulation from left to right, are: *Sibi Jataka* or the story of the pigeon, on the wall of the front aisle between the main doorway and the window to its left; A PALACE SCENE, above the window on the wall of the front aisle to the left of the main doorway; A BIKSHU AT A PALACE DOOR, on the wall of the front aisle between the window and the small door to the left of the main entrance; A PALACE SCENE, on the left wall of the front aisle; *Sankhapala Jataka* or the story of the serpent, on the back wall of the left-hand aisle; THE DANCING GIRL WITH MUSICIANS, *Mahajanaka Jataka*, on the back wall of the left-hand aisle above the door of the second cell; THE RAJA GOING OUT TO ATTEND THE HERMIT'S SERMON, *Mahajanaka Jataka*, on the wall of the left aisle; A RAJA GOING OUT ON HORSEBACK, *Mahajanaka Jataka*, on the back wall of the left-hand aisle; THE SHIPWRECK, *Mahajanaka Jataka*, on the back wall of the left-hand aisle; LUSTRATION AND RENUNCIATION, *Mahajanaka Jataka*, on the wall of the back aisle to the left of the antechamber; FOUR HEADS ON A SALVER, the story of Amara Devi, on the wall of the back

aisle to the left of the antechamber; BODHISATTVA PADMAPANI, on the back wall of the inner aisle to the left of the antechamber; THE TEMPTATION OF THE BUDDHA, on the left-hand wall of the antechamber; BODHISATTVA AVALOKITESVARA, on the back wall of the antechamber to the right of the door to the shrine; THE MIRACLE OF SRAVASTI, on the right-hand wall of the antechamber; OFFERING

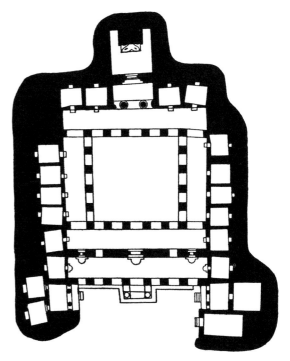

Figure 15   Plan of *Cave I*

LOTUS FLOWERS TO THE BODHISATTVA, on the back wall of the inner aisle to the right of the antechamber; *Campeya Jataka* or the story of a serpent king, on the back wall of the inner aisle; A PALACE SCENE, not identified, on the right-hand wall of the front aisle; A COURT SCENE, known as the Persian Embassy, on the wall of the front aisle on the right of the main entrance; A BACCHANALIAN SCENE with decorative motifs, on the ceiling; THE FIGHTING BULLS, on the capital of the second pillar in the left-hand corner of the hall.

NOTES ON THE PLATES

THE PRINCE AND HIS CONSORT (Pl. 28) and THE WAILING WOMEN (Pl. 24) are reproduced in colour for the first time. They are details from the *Sibi Jataka*. In Buddhist literature several stories are attributed to the charitable Prince Sibi; but the full " pigeon and hawk " anecdote, with scales for weighing an equivalent weight of flesh, is not to be found

except in later works such as *Sutralankara* or the *Bodhisatt-vavadana-kalpa-lata*. The story in CAVE 1 is depicted in three episodes on the wall of the front aisle, between the main doorway and the window to the left of it.

The first episode shows Prince Sibi in a palace surrounded by ladies of the court when the pigeon alights in his lap to seek refuge. Towards the right there is a pavilion containing the detail THE PRINCE AND HIS CONSORT. The Prince, wearing a high crown and a string of pearls across his shoulder, seems to be in a dilemma, while his consort, of greenish complexion, looks at him with curiosity. The connection of this couple with the story has not been established, but possibly they are yet another example of the *mithuna* figures which are so popular at Ajanta. The second and main episode begins immediately to the right of this pavilion. In this scene the Raja is standing by the side of the scales and appears to be on the point of sacrificing his own flesh to save the life of the pigeon. The three lovely figures in THE WAILING WOMEN are among the five figures on the right-hand side of the Raja; they are lamenting at the sight of Bodhisattva's ordeal. These figures, set against the green leaves of a *pipal* tree beyond which the vermilion horizon can be seen, produce a pleasing colour pattern. The conventional flattened perspective (*animnonnata*) of restricted tonal colour scale has been produced by deeply demarcating plain surfaces of pure primary colours. This style appears to have had considerable influence on the hasty, summary technique of drawing and colouring in contemporary art. The third episode, which is painted below the two just mentioned, is damaged almost beyond recognition; but a few fragments show that it is the climax in which the gods, human beings, animals and birds are rejoicing at the Raja's success.

The detail, A DANCING GIRL IN A PALACE SCENE (Pl. 21) is also reproduced in colour for the first time. It is from an unidentified palace scene which is painted on the left wall of the front aisle. The frieze is much damaged, and to give a better idea of it a tracing by Syed Ahmad is reproduced (Fig. 2). The Raja and his consort, in whose court this dance is performed, are apparently Nagas, since they have halos of cobra-hoods over their heads. Nagas are spirits that are said to dwell in ant-hills, pools, lakes and rivers. They generally appear in the form of serpents, and in Buddhist mythology are also represented as anchorites and kings in an invisible world called Nagaloka.

The crowded scene, composed of beautifully attired ladies of the court, female attendants, dwarfs and other courtiers, is typical of the late period; but unlike many of the other figures drawn on this wall, the principal dancer is sketched in extremely graceful curves, with long sweeping brush-strokes, creating a perfect rhythm and balance. The silky shine of her blue jacket is complemented by her pinkish complexion, and her bangles and coiffure are depicted with great care. The colour scheme of clear blue, deep purple-brown, rich malachite-green with touches of clear red, is very beautiful. Although she is drawn in the *paravrtta* attitude of the *Vishnudharmottara*, this conventional formula has not deprived the dancer of her fascinating graceful movement.

THE DANCING GIRL WITH MUSICIANS (Pl. 47) is one of the well-known scenes from the *Mahajanaka Jataka*, which is painted on the wall of the left aisle. It is identified with the episode in which Sivali used a group of dancing girls in an attempt to dissuade Mahajanaka from his resolve to renounce the world. The event is narrated thus : " Queen Sivali sent for seven hundred concubines and said to them,

' It is a long time, four full months, since we last beheld the King Mahajanaka. We shall see him today; do you all adorn yourselves and put forth your graces and blandishments and try to entangle him in the snares of passion.' Attended by them all arrayed and adorned, she ascended the palace to see the King, but although she met him coming down, she knew him not, and thinking that it was a Pacceka-Buddha come to instruct the King, she made a salutation and stood on one side; and the Bodhisattva came down from the palace " (Cowell). Unlike A DANCING GIRL IN A PALACE SCENE, the principal dancer here is attired in a long jacket with full sleeves of a different colour from her close-fitting blouse. Her striped skirt is loose and long, allowing her full freedom of movement. The *arsi* or thumb-ring set with a miniature mirror, the *karanphul* or ear-rings with elaborate design, and the *sarasri* or headdress consisting of strings of gold beads or pearls are all carefully depicted, and the dancer's plaits are ingeniously entwined with flowers. She is surrounded by a group of five musicians; two are playing cymbals, one a pair of *dhole* or drums, another a *mirdang* or a double drum with a narrow ring in the middle, and the fifth a kind of guitar. The costumes, the hair styles, the shape of the eyes and the general atmosphere all epitomize the final phase in the development of the Ajanta style of painting.

The two masterpieces BODHISATTVA PADMAPANI (Pl. 25) and BODHISATTVA AVALOKITESVARA (Pl. 26) have been reproduced in colour many times, but no collection of Ajanta painting can be complete without these *chef-d'œuvres* of Indian art. In the early period the term *Bodhisattva* referred to every member of the *Sangha* or Holy Order, but later, as the religion became more sophisticated, it was restricted to those who possessed extraordinary virtues. Five of these Bodhisattvas were considered to be divine and affiliated to Dhyani Buddhas and their female counterparts, Shaktis. Padmapani, or " the One with a lotus in his hand," is one of the divine Bodhisattvas and he is affiliated to the Dhyani Buddha Amitabha.

According to the Buddhist scriptures, Padmapani has been performing the duty of Buddha since the disappearance of Gautama, and he will continue to do so until Maitreya, who is now in the Tushita heaven, comes back to this world. Similarly, Avalokitesvara (earlier identified as Vajrapani) is regarded as having emanated from Amitabha and his Shakti Pandara. He is the most esteemed Bodhisattva of the Mahayana pantheon, being styled Sangharatna, or " Jewel of the Order." This figure is painted on the back wall of the inner aisle, to the right of the antechamber, symmetrical with BODHISATTVA PADMAPANI on the other side of the antechamber. These two paintings show clearly that by the close of the Ajanta tradition northern and southern influences were freely intermingled. By virtue of Ajanta's relationship to Gandhara and Greco-Roman art and contacts with the Kushano-Iranians, the northern influence is still predominant in BODHISATTVA PADMAPANI, which has Aryan features and fair skin, while the dark skin, round face and fuller lips that were prominent in the Ajanta paintings of the pre-Christian era reappear in the Deccani-type ethnic structure of the BODHISATTVA AVALOKITESVARA. The more elaborate jewellery of the AVALOKITESVARA also reflect southern customs and fashions. In the drawing and colouring the artists seem to have used similar techniques. There is, however, a greater relief effect in the drawing of the AVALOKITESVARA, chiefly because of the larger area of greenish background to the figure.

Through the extraordinary confidence of the line and the softness of the shading the countenances reflect a lyrical and pensive abstraction. The flawless, opalescent smoothness of the skin, the beautiful proportion of body to face, and the eyes half-closed in meditation radiate celestial beauty and purity. Textures and muscular structure are scarcely indicated so that the figures symbolize the divine anatomy of Supernatural Beings.

Plate 78   A detail from the ceiling of *Cave 1*

The restraint of the sacred style of painting in the Bodhisattvas is beautifully balanced by the lively background and the warm atmosphere of the secular scene. The background is infused with the colours of the luxuriant foliage of the areca palms and the Ashoka trees, the strong red squares like pillars and cross-pieces which are a convention for the ridges of hills, the clear blue of the bird's feathers, and a variety of other colours which enliven the drapery and jewellery and even the skins of the men and women. As Laurence Binyon wrote : " The Bodhisattva attended by his consort on one side and a vigilant guard on the other, and with the background of mingling curves and jutting angles, where the eye, losing itself at first, discovers by degrees one form and one detail after another; here it is the gleam of flesh where a woman leans among foliage on her lover's shoulder, and a peacock is crying beside his mate, and, more obscure, a monkey plays intently. There, shapes of supernatural beings begin to appear, some floating through the air, others playing music on instruments; the relaxed posture of a woman reclining in her lover's arms takes the eye among more shadowy forms. Human and divine are mingled; it is as if all were rooted in the rich soil of life; and contemplating the fresco one has something like the feeling produced by gazing into an intricate depth of flowering foliage, leaf behind leaf bough behind bough, when, lingering till the fall of the dusk, one may see the colours of the blooms retire into themselves, yet still burn unequally with a kind of secret glow."

On the right hand side of BODHISATTVA PADMAPANI and below the *gandharvas* which are flying in the air, the MITHUNA FIGURES (Pl. 27) are watching the Great Being from their hill retreat as they sit in an amorous mood. This detail should be compared with THE PRINCE AND HIS CONSORT (Pl. 28), which depicts the same subject in the same cave, but provides a complete contrast in the manner of drawing and colouring. While THE PRINCE AND HIS CONSORT consists of flat irregular planes put together like a jig-saw puzzle, delighting us with the geometrically conceived human figures, the MITHUNA FIGURES retain the softness and roundness of the limbs, demarcated only by a slight deepening of the colours along the edges. The contours in the latter are so natural and so perfect that they give an exact impression of shape even in the most difficult foreshortenings of limbs. These two details are good examples of the *animnonnata* and *nimnonnata* treatment of painting respectively.

SHAKTI PANDARA (Pl. 36) is another famous painting at Ajanta. In the opinion of Yazdani it is one of the finest works of art in the world. Popularly known as *The Black Princess*, it is probably a representation of Amitabha's *Shakti Pandara*. Its fine modelling, exquisite ornamentation, tranquillity and thoughtfulness are beautifully brought out by the dark complexion against a lighter background. Certainly there is no other portrait at Ajanta with such perfect eyes; the hazel-brown of the pupils and the red spots in the corners of the eyes radiate an astonishing natural friendliness. It is truly an unusual painting, considering the late period to which it belongs, when the elongated and exaggerated eyes of a declining art were already in vogue.

Like the two famous Bodhisattvas PADMAPANI and AVALOKITESVARA, LUSTRATION AND RENUNCIATION (Pl. 20) is among the finest paintings of the late period. The frieze is another example of the way in which the sacred and the secular manners met in delightful equality, combining the restraint of the representations of the Bodhisattvas with the lyricism of the paintings of women. Renunciation is a favourite theme of the *Jatakas*; this painting is generally considered to refer to Prince Mahajanaka.

Prince Mahajanaka is shown here squatting on a throne while two servants are pouring water over him from fluted metal pitchers. As was the custom, " he bathed himself with sixteen pitchers of perfumed water and adorned himself in all his magnificence." On the Raja's left are three women attendants who are painted in different colours and are extremely graceful in their act of aiding Mahajanaka with his royal dress and ornaments. Even more enchanting are the two women on the Prince's right. The elegance of their poses and movements can be compared with the famous " Hariti Shrine " votaries. A lady with a tray whose dark complexion is beautifully balanced by the red column towards her left and the fair complexion of the woman who is stooping in front of her to pick up a load from the head of a dwarf servant, displays movement so free and poise so graceful that its equal is hard to find. Both these women are dressed in garments which are almost transparent. The various skin-colours and the red of the columns of the pavilion are harmoniously blended against the dull olive green of areca-nut palm leaves, producing a delightful colour-pattern.

The architecture of the pavilion in which the scene is enacted is typical of the late period. The red pillars are fixed at their bases in a frame of wood which rests on rampant tiger and hyena-heads, and the capitals are painted blue by a dot or stipple technique. The hyena-heads are a favourite decorative motif at this period and can also be seen on the façade of the main entrance to this cave.

ONE OF MARA'S ATTENDANTS (Pl. 68) is a detail from the TEMPTATION OF THE BUDDHA BY MARA which is on the left of the antechamber. It is reproduced in colour here for the first time. The portrait shows one of the attendants in Mara's army who attempted in vain to distract Gautama from his austere way of life. The beauty of this painting, which is probably one of the earliest in this cave, and its artistic quality compare with the classic wall in CAVE XVII depicting the *Simhala Avadana*. Here too the artist's vision is projected over an entire wall, and the activities of Mara, the Buddhist devil, are interpreted with a vigour and liveliness which has few parallels. The Buddha's figure, serene and calm, is painted in the centre of the wall, and he is surrounded by a fantastic variety of monsters and witches. Around the Buddha, who sits in *bhumi-sparsa-mudra*, or Earth Touching attitude, there is a group of seven young damsels whose pretty features, graceful poses and soft facial expressions have been justly compared to the women in Raphael's paintings. Especially beautiful are the two women one on either side of the Buddha. They are apparently two of Mara's three enchanting daughters, Desire, Pleasure and Passion, who unsuccessfully tried every means of seduction.

On the wall on which the Buddha is being subjected to spiritual stress and physical strain by all kinds of threats and temptations, a tiny bush of LEAVES AND FLOWERS (Pl. 14), painted in one corner, is symbolic of a ray of hope and the ultimate conquest of the self. It forms part of the sophisticated repertory of flowers at Ajanta. Ajanta was undoubtedly the source from which an enormous wealth of plants and flowers were introduced into China, Japan, Korea and the countries of South-East Asia. The leaves and flowers seen here are the Ashoka (Saraca Indica), a small tree with long green leaves bearing scarlet or orange blossoms which, it was said, would only flower if kicked by a beautiful woman. The other favourite plants are the areca-nut palm, the tall Sirica, the orange-flowered Kadamba and the red Kimsuka. In many panels of the walls and on the ceilings there is an incredible variety of Indian fruits and flowers combined with fanciful animal, bird and human forms. Even if the rendering of Ajanta trees and flowers is more "solid" and their arrangement is more static, nevertheless they blend beautifully with the other subjects.

A QUEEN IN A PALACE SCENE (Pl. 17) has not been identified but it is apparently a scene from a *Jataka*. This figure in front of a Raja and another detail, THE WOMAN WITH THE LOTUS (Pl. 16), which is just below the Queen, are certainly of a late period. They represent what is termed the full Baroque, which shows a decline marked by ana-

Plate 79   A detail from *Lustration and Renunciation*

tomical distortions comparable with Pala art. Compared with the fifth century paintings, the classical poses and decorative elements are exaggerated, displaying many similarities with the late Bagh frescoes and with the Jain frescoes at Sittanavasal in South India of the early Pallava period. The peculiarities of the style are the heavy heads, elongated eyes, excessively large mouths, thin legs, and the superfluous hand gestures. In addition the composition became careless, perhaps because of mass production, and the finish of the paintings was summary.

THE CHAURI BEARER (Pl. 23), here published in colour for the first time, is a detail from what is commonly known as THE PERSIAN EMBASSY. This frieze continues to be a subject of controversy among scholars, as many of the characters depicted appear to be foreigners. While some consider it to represent the Embassy of the Persian King Khosru, others attribute it to the court of the Chalukyan

Raja Pulakesin at the beginning of the seventh century; there are yet other scholars who consider this painting to be a scene from another *Jataka* which has not been identified. There is, however, little doubt that the foreigners bear a resemblance to the people of Turkestan and other countries to the north-west of India, with whom the Ajanta artists must have been familiar even in the early centuries of the Christian era through the Sakas, who were established in Saurashtra and Malwa. As this detail shows, the style of the frieze links it also with the wall-paintings in the later Buddhist ruins of Chinese Turkestan.

The painting shows a court scene in which the Raja is squatting on the throne with his legs crossed and leaning on a pillow. He is attended by numerous officers, dignitaries and female attendants. In the middle of the assembly there are three foreigners wearing long coats (*qaba*), one of whom is about to present a pearl decoration to the monarch; the other two seem to be waiting their turn. There are a number of male and female attendants wearing a variety of colourful clothes and holding objects in their hands such as *chauris*, fans, jewel-caskets and round metal vessels. At the head of them is an imposing official holding a long green staff. Possibly he is the court chamberlain.

Some parts of this frieze (such as THE CHAURI BEARER) are executed with fine brush work, but on the whole, despite the size of the figures and the admirable grouping, the painting has little special merit. It is a product of the late period when the art had begun to languish.

THE FIGHTING BULLS (Pl. 6), compared by Laurence Binyon with a famous drawing of the same subject by Toba Sojo, the great Japanese draftsman of the twelfth century, is one of the most forceful and vigorous drawings at Ajanta. The two bulls convey a tense fury, and this effect is enhanced by the delineation of their bodies in identical postures; their heads are lowered, muscles contracted, tails raised, and the curves of their necks and humps are protruded. We know of the same subject depicted in the Bhaja Cave, and one thousand years later a representation of two bulls engaged in combat painted in Mahal-i-Khas in Fatehpur Sikri, but neither of these paintings reaches the power of pictorial expression attained at Ajanta.

THE RECLINING WOMAN (Pl. 33) is one of the many beautiful *mithuna* figures which are drawn without any respect for the Greek ideal; nor did any detailed anatomical knowledge interfere with the artist's interpretation of the supple body. The lovely, slender figure is not disguised by the transparent garment. Unlike the Italian painters of the *quattrocento* such as Pollaiuolo and Signorelli, to whom the naked body was a revelation, Ajanta artists regarded the unclothed human body as no more than a part of everyday life.

Also in contrast to European painting, the artists of Ajanta did not paint religious subjects on ceilings. The reason for this is not known, but apparently it was considered easier for the devotees to "read" the *Jatakas* and other scenes depicting the life of the Master on the walls. Thus the entire ceiling of each cave at Ajanta was covered with decorative motifs: birds and animals of exquisite design, colourful flowers and fruits among foliage, human beings in fantastic forms and wonderfully varied geometric patterns.

CAVE TWO

This *vihara*, although slightly smaller, has a similar plan to that of CAVE 1. The veranda is 2.4 meters wide and has a length of 14.1 meters. The façades of the chapels at each end of the veranda are carved with figures of the Naga kings and their attendants, the portly Ganas. The congregation hall is about 14.5 meters square and the roof is supported by twelve massive, elaborately-carved pillars. There are ten cells off four corridors, three off the right and left corridors and two each off the corridors at the front and rear. The shrine is 4.2 by 3.3 meters and contains a large figure of the Buddha in the *dharmacakra* or teaching attitude. The doorway of the shrine and the antechamber are profusely carved. On either side of the antechamber is a chapel, the entrances of which are adorned with delicately-carved pillars.

The main surviving paintings in the cave are: ARHATS, KINNARAS, and other mythical beings adoring the Bo-dhisattva, on the back wall of the veranda to the left of the door; VOTARIES BRINGING OFFERINGS and INDRA AND THE FOUR YAKSHAS, on the back wall of the veranda to the right of the doorway; NYMPHS AND FLORAL DESIGNS on the ceiling of the veranda; THE EXILE OF A LADY (not identified) on the left wall of the chapel to the right end of the veranda; *Mahahamsa Jataka* or the story of the golden goose, on the left wall of the front gallery; YAKSHAS AND YAKSHINIS on the pilaster between the front and the left galleries; THE BIRTH OF THE BUDDHA (in several scenes) on the wall of the left-hand corridor; VOTARIES BRINGING OFFERINGS, on the left-hand wall of the chapel to the left of the antechamber; DRAGONS, GEESE, and other decorative motifs, on the ceiling of the chapel to the left of the antechamber; THE BUDDHA (in various poses) on the wall of the back corridor between the antechamber and the left chapel; THE BODHISATTVA MAITREYA on the front wall of the shrine, to the left of the door; THE BUDDHA (in various poses) on the right and the left walls of the shrine; CHERUBS, FLORAL DESIGNS and other decorative motifs, on the ceiling of the shrine; THE BODHISATTVA AVALOKITESVARA, on the wall of the back corridor, between the antechamber and the right-hand chapel; VOTARIES BRINGING OFFERINGS, on the left-hand wall of the chapel to the right of the antechamber; VOTARIES BRINGING OFFERINGS TO BODHISATTVA PADMAPANI, on the right-hand wall of the chapel to the right of the antechamber; *Vidhurapandita Jataka*, on the wall of the right-hand corridor; PURNA AVADANA, or the story of a sea voyage, on the wall between the doors of the second and the third cells of the right-hand corridor; A PALACE SCENE (not identified) on the right-hand side of the door of the third cell in the right-hand corridor; A LADY KNEELING AT THE FEET OF A RAJA, on the right-hand wall of the front corridor; A BODHISATTVA (in teaching attitude) on the right-hand wall of the front gallery; DECORATIVE DESIGNS on the ceilings of the front and rear corridors and the main hall; and NAGAS, GANAS AND OTHER MYTHICAL BEINGS on the pedestals of the columns of the hall.

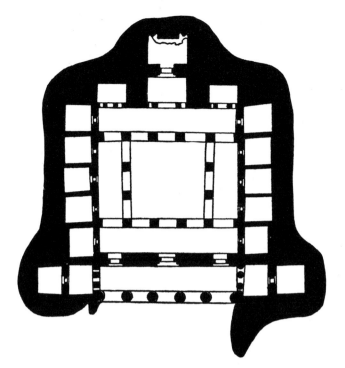

Figure 16   Plan of *Cave II*

NOTES ON THE PLATES

THE LOTUS IN THE WONDERFUL LAKE OF BRAHMADATTA (Pl. 43) and A GATE IN KING BRAHMADATTA'S PALACE (Pl. 44) are two unusual details reproduced in colour for the first time. The lotus lake scenes are on either side of the cell door and the palace scene is above it. The style is one in which the masses are refined and transformed to produce an orderly pattern composed of geometrically-conceived shapes. The version of the *Mahahamsa Jataka* has four episodes. The first episode depicts a lake covered with lotuses in which the fowler with a companion is laying his snares to catch the golden geese. In the second episode the two divine birds are instructing the Raja of Benares and his consort Khema in the mysteries of the Law. The Goose King is sitting on a throne beside his chief adviser Sumukha. The third episode, which is absent in the *Jataka*, is also a court scene, in which the golden goose has miraculously assumed human form while teaching the Law to the Raja and his court. The fourth episode is similar to the first, showing the lotus lake with different kinds of beautiful lotus flowers; Queen Khema is seen watching the graceful movements of the golden geese, which are now free to live as they like.

WOMEN ON THE BALCONY (Pl. 34), also reproduced in colour for the first time, is a detail from a group of six women painted on the left wall of the chapel to the left of the antechamber. The figure in the forefront of the group is resting her elbow elegantly on the parapet, looking at the people below. This is among the few figures in this chapel which merit some attention because, although the drawing is crude by classical standards, the long brush sweep with which the right arm has been drawn is reminiscent of the method employed in the drawing of animals such as THE MONKEY BENEATH A PALAS TREE (Pl. 3). The

other paintings in this chapel are generally of poor quality, and completely different from the masterpieces in the "Hariti Shrine" to the right of the antechamber. The two chapels have the same dimensions, and the same subject is depicted in both, but the painting in this chapel is broken up into compartments so that the procession of votaries, instead of moving in an idyllic open landscape, is crowded within a series of pillared verandas and balconies. The surviving pieces here show at least twenty-six persons as compared with half that number on the "Hariti Shrine" wall. Except for the women on the balconies, all the votaries are drawn as almost the same size and are clustered in pillared compartments, conveying a feeling that is the antithesis of the atmosphere of classical tranquillity. Whether these two chapels were excavated at the same time is difficult to tell, but as far as the paintings are concerned, the possibility of a considerable time gap between the two cannot be ruled out.

Rightly compared by William Rothenstein and Roger Fry with Botticelli's *Primavera*, the classical style of Ajanta painting at its finest is undoubtedly represented by the two superb panels, VOTARIES WITH OFFERINGS (Pl. 31 and 32). The admirable composition of these two panels of identical size is constructed around the five main figures in such a way that they occupy a major portion of the wall; the other figures are about half the size and occupy the four corners. The scene set is a landscape of rocks and gardens and admirably creates an atmosphere of carefree tranquillity, as the lovely women proceed with gentle swaying movements towards the shrine. Unobtrusive modelling and calm linear harmony, combined with a restrained use of red tints for the women, is balanced against the greens of the banana leaves. In this symphony of Ajanta colour and composition,

THE DOVE (Pl. 4), from the "Hariti Shrine," shows remarkable confidence of draftsmanship. As in the drawing of the trees and flowers of Ajanta, the rendering, though solid and firm, has not destroyed a wonderful illusion of lightness. It is generally accepted that the "Hariti Shrine" panels belong to the early fifth century. C. Fabri, however, having compared the shrine with a long architrave from the temple of Garhwa, in the district of Allahabad, thinks that the panels can be dated to about 400. The Garhwa relievo has been dated by no less than five inscriptions to 417, and Fabri dates the Ajanta votaries, displaying slightly less bending of the body, to a few years earlier than the Garhwa relievo.

For pose, expression and movement, it is difficult to match the episodes of the *Vidhurapandita Jataka* on the wall of the right-hand corridor of this cave. Some delightful details are reproduced here in colour for the first time. The sequence of events appears to be different from that of the *Jataka*. On the left we see Puranaka showing the magnificent jewel to King Dhananjaya, who looks at him sceptically as he sits on the throne covered with cloth with a zig-zag design. The drawing of the King has a grace of style and clarity of expression obtained chiefly by a firm outline and the use of highlights and shading. The gestures of Puranaka's hands and those of the people around him effectively convey the animated discussion leading to the contest which, according to the *Jataka*, was witnessed by one hundred kings. The figures of the ladies of the court, including the one who is on the King's right (probably his consort), show a fine sense of proportion in drawing and colouring. Puranaka is seen stooping at the extreme right of the group, with the jewel in the palm of his hand. The drawing of his figure, and of his Sindhi horse behind him, is done with a delicate feeling and considerable skill. Moving towards the right, in an adjoining room of the palace, Dhanajaya is shown gambling with Puranaka. The King is shown at the moment when he has just thrown the dice on to the board, which is prominently placed in the middle of the group. The next scene to the right is apparently set in the Naga world, where we see Vidhurapandita seated on a low stool, instructing and initiating the Naga King Varuna in the Law of the Buddha. Behind him is Puranaka, who is seated on a cushion of intricate design. The attitude of the Naga King and his profound respect are excellently conveyed by his joined hands and slight bow. The halo of five serpent-hoods, besides indicating his status, create an atmosphere of mystery. Outside the pillared halls can be seen Puranaka's Sindhi horse (which has been painted twice to show his descent from the air and his landing). To the right we see the Queen on a balcony, engaged in conversation with a young lady. This is probably Vimala's private apartment, and here she is shown discussing with Irandati the prospect of her marriage with Puranaka. Below this balcony there is another on which the Bodhisattva with a lotus flower in his hand is seen in conversation with Vimala. The steps and balustrades of the balconies are interesting examples of the architecture of the period. To the right of THE GAME OF DICE is an assembly of Varuna's kinsmen, friends, and other Naga chiefs, whom he is consulting about Puranaka's proposals. In front of the King are two Naga chiefs, one of whom, bearing a single ser-

pent's hood on his head, is squatting on the ground. A NAGA CHIEF (Pl. 41) is one of the finest profiles at Ajanta; the drawing is vigorous, the colour-pattern of the dark olive complexion, jet black hair, reddish background sprinkled with flowers and the soft blues of the ribbon on his neck is charming, and the composition excellent. Another delightful painting in this frieze is a girl in a swing, who has been identified as PRINCESS IRANDATI (Pl. 37). The decorated background and the ropes of the swing adorned with flags, in the midst of which Irandati is seated with her legs outstretched, excellently convey the effect of movement. This painting illustrates a version of the *Jataka* in which the princess, in search of a husband, "gathered all the flowers in the Himalaya which had colour, scent or taste, and having adorned the entire mountain like a precious jewel, she spread a couch of flowers upon it, and, after executing a pleasing dance, she sang a sweet song." Below this sequence of scenes there are others, such as a

Plate 80   A detail from the ceiling of *Cave II*

magnificent royal procession in which Vidhurapandita is seen riding in state on an elephant.

The colourful HORSES IN A PROCESSION (Pl. 39), with its footmen and soldiers armed with short swords and shields painted with dragon heads, is possibly a representation of Vidhurapandita's journey home after his successful sojourn in the Naga world. This lovely frieze is a stylistic paradox in that it exhibits elements from almost all the periods and styles of Ajanta painting, yet the effect is one of rare homogeneity of drawing and colouring. The facial features are almost identical to those in The Raja with his Retinue (Pl. 48); the golden-brown complexions, almost-round faces, small bright eyes, full red lips, and short but pointed noses are familiar from the non-Aryan types depicted in the paintings of the pre-Christian era. Here the women wear veils over their heads and the menfolk elaborate turbans, but the hair-styles with short locks, fringes falling over the foreheads, are identical in the two paintings. There are no bulging body-curves, no cork-screw curls, and the eyes are not elongated; in fact there is none of the exaggeration associated with the late period. There are no Gandhara robes; both men and women are bare above the waist, wearing extremely few ornaments and with their hair adorned chiefly with fresh flowers and a few jewels. The general design of the frieze is well conceived (like the *Simhala Avadana* wall in Cave XVII, with few pillars and without unnecessary compartments).

If we were to assign paintings to successive periods on a pictorial and stylistic basis, the temptation would be to place this frieze in a period somewhat later than The Raja with his Retinue and certainly before the *Simhala Avadana* frieze. But since the people represented in the *Vidhura-pandita* frieze are southern types and it is generally admitted by scholars that, apart from the early period, the appearance of Deccani types is a late development, this proposition is at once invalidated. It is therefore logical to assume that the wall was painted during a period of transition between the classical and the late period. This supposition is supported by the presence of a number of pictorial forms which are either identical with or a combination of features belonging to the classical and late periods. For instance, while some portions of the wall have a classical spatial distribution of the figures, there are other portions which convey a sense of excitement and strain because the figures are unequally held together in an implied tension. This latter tendency is essentially a product of the late period referred to as the Baroque, when activity is introduced into particular sections of the picture, so conferring a crowded feeling on the spatial arrangement. Both these characteristics are seen in The Game of Dice. On the left-hand side, where Puranaka displays the magnificent jewel to King Dhananjaya in order to induce him to gamble, the clustering of the figures is in sharp contrast with the calm linear harmony of the portion depicting Vidhurapandita and Princess Vimala (Pl. 42). While too many figures in a small area indicates a departure from the classical style, yet happily the people retain the classical simplicity of "essential form." The cramming together of the figures has not deprived the men and women of their refined, romantic and sympathetic natures. The most exquisite example of this is the detail of Princess Irandati. This lyrical painting is a sign of emancipation from the ascetism of the sacred style, an emancipation which the Ajanta artists, rightly or wrongly, were struggling to achieve. The same attitude is discernible in the use of colour; the predominant burnt sienna and olive green are now occasionally replaced by bright reds and blues. Here, perhaps, we see the beginning of the preoccupation of the later period when colouring was more often used arbitrarily and was intended solely to please the eye. The unrestrained colours in many pieces—in marked contrast to the sober, pious gestures of the "conventionalists"—reflect the frame of mind of the ebullient new generation of artists, who perhaps set the stage for the inauguration of the Baroque period.

The greater part of the ceiling is destroyed, but enough remains to show the general arrangement and complexity of the design. The area is divided into panels of various shapes and filled with intricate painted designs. A great variety of decorative motifs, such as flowers, fruits, birds, jewellery designs and fantastic geometrical patterns are sometimes bordered by *mithuna* figures. Among flowers the lotus is prominent, and we see here many different kinds, including the large white and blue variety. The fruits are mangos, pomegranates and pineapples, painted as separate bunches or hanging from luxuriant branches. There are also birds, including parrots, geese, ducks and cranes, as well as many kinds of animals which are combined with decorative and fanciful forms. Among the sportive figures are dwarfs, buffoons, jugglers, wine-bibbers, foreigners in strange attire, and so on. Griffiths, in his monumental work Paintings in the Buddhist Cave Temples of Ajanta, has devoted a whole volume to these decorative details.

CAVE SIX

This two-storied *vihara* at Ajanta is assigned to the fifth to sixth centuries A.D. Its basement contains sixteen simple octagonal pillars, without capitals, dividing the hall into three aisles. Through a lavishly carved doorway, the central aisle leads into the shrine, where on a lion throne is carved the Buddha. There are ten cells on the lower storey. A staircase in the veranda on the right of the entrance climbs to the porch of the upper storey, where on both sides there are single cells with antechambers. The main hall of the upper storey has twelve pillars and two chapels on either side. The corridor of the main hall passes through an antechamber and ends in the shrine where an impressive figure of the Buddha is carved with flying *apsarasas* and attendants.

The principal surviving paintings on the lower storey of the *vihara* are: The Buddha in the Teaching Attitude, on the left-hand wall of the antechamber; Dvarapalas and

A FEMALE VOTARY, on the back wall of the antechamber, on either side of the entrance to the shrine; THE TEMPTATION OF THE BUDDHA, on the right-hand wall of the antechamber.

The main paintings in the upper storey are : A BIKSHU, near the feet of the Buddha carved on the left-hand wall of the antechamber; DVARAPALAS AND PAIRS OF MALE AND FEMALE FIGURES, on the jambs and side-walls of the doorway of the chapel at the right-hand end of the front corridor; THE MIRACLE OF STRAVASTI, on the right-hand wall of the chapel in the front corridor; A SKETCH OF A MAN, on the right-hand wall of the antechamber on the left side of the porch; and MINIATURE ANIMALS DRAWINGS, on the ceiling of the right-hand chapel.

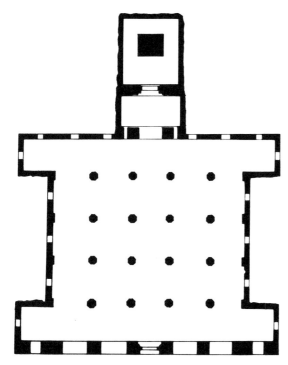

Figure 17   Plan of the lower storey of *Cave VI*

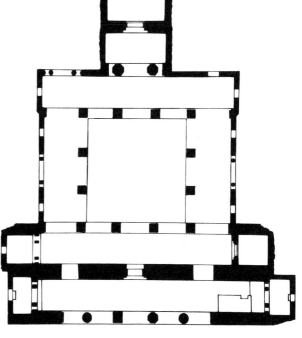

Figure 18   Plan of the upper storey of *Cave VI*

NOTES ON THE PLATES

The walls of the upper storey, like those of the ground floor, were once all covered with paintings, but now, unfortunately, with the exception of a few fragments the colours have completely perished. The most interesting surviving piece is A BHIKSHU WITH A LOTUS (Pl. 74), which is drawn in a firm black outline and coloured in only two tones. The Bhikshu is seen with a metal censer in his right hand while in his left he holds three lotus flowers representing the *triratna*, denoting the Buddha, the Order and the Law. The fingers and toes have been painted with great care and the posture makes a perfect picture of devotion and dedication. The line rhythm of this image and simple decorative colour pattern are said to have influenced Chinese painting of the T'ang Dynasty. Its ideals are still preserved in the painted plaster bas-reliefs in southern Indian temples and in Nepalese woodcuts.

Reproduced in colour for the first time, A BUDDHIST NUN (Pl. 45), is an exquisite detail from *The Great Miracle of Sravasti*, which is painted on the right wall of the chapel in the front corridor of the upper storey. This legend tells of the Buddha's miraculous powers which he displayed in the presence of King Prasenajit of Sravasti in order to confound the heretical teachers. Of the many miracles shown, one is that of the Buddha's appearing simultaneously in different places.

The pose in which the Nun is drawn is unique : there is no other surviving piece at Ajanta showing such a posture. In fact all the images depicted on this much defaced wall are among the finest examples of painting of the late period. The refinement of feature and expression in these figures has prompted some art critics to compare them with the finest works of Italian artists of the fourteenth and fifteenth centuries. The mastery of line which created the Buddha in this frieze is also seen in the elegant figure of the Nun, whose right hand raised above her head shows an extraordinary ease and confidence of draftsmanship and a perfect sense of proportion.

Another most interesting piece in this shrine, painted on the back wall of the antechamber, is A WOMAN WITH LARGE EAR-RINGS. Unfortunately it is much damaged, but when complete it must surely have been one of the master-pieces of the later style of Ajanta.

THE CALF (Pl. 7), painted on the ceiling of the right chapel in the upper storey of this *vihara*, is here reproduced in colour for the first time. The simple linear style of the animals and birds drawn in simple lines, is reminiscent of the terracotta toys from the Indus Valley civilization of the third millenium B.C. It is worth noting that this style is quite different from that of the sophisticated details of jewellery, the bands and borders of the robes on the *dvar-palas* (door-guardians) and pairs of male and female figures painted on the side-posts and the side-walls of the chapel doorway, at the right-hand side of the front corridor.

CAVE NINE

The plan of this temple is rectangular, and it has an archi-tectural dignity all its own. It has twenty-one octagonal pillars which are about 3 meters high. The interior dimen-sions of the cave are 13.5 meters long, 7 meters wide and 7.1 meters high. The *stupa* carved at the end of the hall has a dome one meter high above a cylindrical base and it is crowned by a square capital representing the reliquary. The *chaitya* has a beautifully decorated façade with a berm-railing, windows and lattice frame. The large figures of the Buddha carved along the sides of the cave are later addi-tions (fifth or sixth century) while the cave was probably excavated in the first century B.C.

The *chaitya* contains paintings of different periods. Some of these belong to the first century B.C., while others are assigned to a period as late as the fourth or fifth century. The main subjects painted are: A NAGA KING WITH HIS ATTENDANTS, on the inner side of the front wall above the left window; A GROUP OF VOTARIES APPROACHING A STUPA, on the left wall; A MONASTERY, on the rear wall towards the left; TWO SCENES FROM THE LIFE OF THE BUDDHA, on the rear wall to the right; THE ANIMAL FRIEZE, above the pillars of the nave on the left-hand side; and BUDDHAS (in various attitudes), on the triforium.

Figure 19   Plan of *Cave IX*

NOTES ON THE PLATES

When he copied the paintings with his party of students from the Bombay School of Art in 1875-1885, John Griffiths revealed several new figures. Among these were the two Bhikshus which are painted on the inner side of the front wall. The heads of these Bhikshus are similar to THE BODHISATTVA (Pl. 67). Assigned to the late fourth or early fifth century A.D., this style of painting is almost identical with that of THE BUDDHA, which is painted on the triforium above pillar VI on the right side. The beauty of the draw-ing and colouring is in harmony with the attitudes of medi-tation and contemplation. The profound inner experience emanating from the half-closed eyes of these figures seems to light up their faces. The bright red parasols and Ashoka trees painted against a dull greenish background create a delightful autumnal effect. These are among the earliest examples of a style which, having digested varied influences, still retained its essential simplicity and naturalness; the iconography and decorative forms of these paintings were in turn transmitted to Champa and Cambodia, the Northern Wei in China, and early Buddhist Japan.

Of the paintings from the earliest periods, there are none which can now be reproduced photographically. Two sketches, A GROUP OF VOTARIES APPROACHING A STUPA (Fig. 5) and THE STUPA (Fig. 6) are included in this volume to give an idea of the ribbon-like composition of the early paintings. Figure 5 shows a group of sixteen votaries who are approaching the door of a Stupa. The variety of their postures and gestures and their hair-styles intertwined with strips of cloth are remarkable. The men's headgear, con-sisting of a top-knot with elaborately plaited terminations protuding over the forehead, and their decorative waist-bands are also extremely interesting. The grouping of the figures is natural, and is typical of the painting of this period.

The sketch depicting THE STUPA (Fig. 6) clearly shows the typical architecture of the first centuries B.C. The stupa is enclosed by four walls, which have two gates. The gate on the left side has a barrel-shaped roof with timber rafters, like that of the contemporary caves at Karle and Bedsa. The gateway on the right side is in the style of the Sanchi gates, and this painting is therefore thought by some to be contemporaneous. In the middle stands the Stupa under a number of umbrellas, which are Buddhist emblems of dignity and sanctity. Outside the enclosure can be seen the devotees and a banyan tree.

CAVE TEN

On the strength of an inscription this *chaitya* is considered to be the oldest of the caves and has been assigned to the first half of the second century B.C. It has an impressive, lofty ceiling and a spacious nave; altogether it is 29 meters long, 12.1 meters wide and 11 meters high. Thirty-nine pillars, which divide the aisles from the nave, support an entablature which rests on the vault of the barrel-shaped roof. The pillars are 12 meters high and lean inward in imitation of the posts of the ancient bamboo structures, to support the weight of the curvilinear roofs made of wooden rafters and cross-beams.

The *chaitya*, like CAVE IX, contains paintings of different periods. On the strength of two inscriptions the oldest are thought to be roughly contemporaneous with the excavation of the cave in the second century B.C. The principal paintings in the *chaitya* are : THE ARRIVAL OF A RAJA WITH HIS RETINUE, on the rear wall of the left aisle; THE ROYAL PARTY WORSHIPPING AT A STUPA, on the left-hand wall behind pillars nine to eleven; THE ROYAL PARTY PASSING THROUGH A GATEWAY, on the left-hand wall behind pillars eleven to fifteen; *Syama Jataka*, on the right-hand wall behind pillars eleven to fifteen; *Shaddanta Jataka*, or the story of the six-tusked elephant, on the back wall of the right-hand aisle behind pillars two to twelve; and VARIOUS FIGURES OF THE BUDDHA, painted on different pillars.

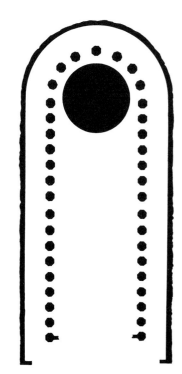

Figure 20   Plan of *Cave X*

NOTES ON THE PLATES

One of the painted inscriptions to give us a date (see notes on the Cave, above) is thought to be connected with THE RAJA WITH HIS RETINUE (Pl. 48), undoubtedly one of the most significant paintings at Ajanta. In this painting the Raja, accompanied by ten ladies and a child, is seen approaching the Bodhi tree, which is represented here by a *pipal* tree decorated with banners. The women, nearly naked from the waist upward, are wearing simple ornaments comprising earrings, necklaces, armlets and bangles. Specially notable are the ivory bangles of conch-shell (examples of which have been found in excavations at Maski, Paithan and Kondapur) which cover almost the entire forearm. These are still in fashion among the Lambadi tribes in the Deccan. The women's hair-styles vary from the highly elaborate to the quite simple. On their foreheads a few ladies have circular colour-marks such as Indian women still wear today. Another notable feature of the dress of this period is the large scarves or veils over the women's heads. In the later period these are conspicuously absent, perhaps because of the influence of the North on the

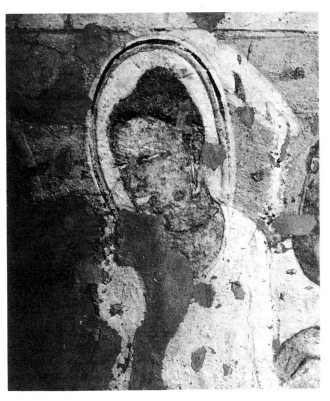

Plate 81   The Bodhisattva: *Cave X*

even earlier. At Ajanta the darker skins and non-Aryan features completely disappeared for quite some time, and reappeared again possibly in the second half of the fifth century.

Another important frieze in this cave is the one representing the *Syama Jataka*. It is impossible to take good photographs of this largely-effaced painting, so we must be content with sketches (Fig. 3 and Fig. 4). The two episodes of the *Syama Jataka* are drawn in a style which is apparently close to that of Sunga art, representing types which are somewhat similar to those on the railings of Bharhut. The faces are still conventional, but are expressive, and the painting as a whole effectively conveys the tense atmosphere of the hunting scene. Another notable frieze illustrated here by a line-drawing is THE BODHISATTVA AND HIS HERD OF ELEPHANTS (Fig. 7). It is an excellent picture, full of love for life and nature, in which the artist has made full use of his proficiency in the drawing of animals and birds, a tradition which he inherited from the Indus Valley civilization of the third millennium B.C. Similarly, THE QUEEN FAINTS AT THE SIGHT OF THE TUSKS (Fig. 8) which was probably painted half a century or more later than the others, shows a maturity of drawing in the Andhra style. The elegance of the figures and facial expression reflect late Sanchi sculpture.

The paintings on the *dagoba* and the aisles have almost completely perished, but there are some exquisite survivals of the Buddha and Bodhisattvas on the pillars, as well as some lovely creeper and floral designs, especially on the fifth, sixth and seventh pillars to the right of the door. The standing Buddha is generally shown in the *bhumisparsa mudra* or Earth-Touching attitude, while the standing images are drawn in *dharmacakra* or the Teaching attitude. Northern influences are clearly reflected in these representations, where the togas, hair styles and facial features are quite different from those of the people from the south. This is specially evident in the beautiful painting THE BUDDHA AND THE ONE-EYED MONK (Pl. 54), which is painted on the sixth pillar on the right-hand side of the cave. The Buddha's features are clearly taken from the people from the north, the lyrical quality of the flowing transparent garments falling on the beautifully-moulded, smooth limbs of the Gandhara Buddhas here finds an astonishing echo. The influence of the Hellenic-Gandhara-Indian complex is seen even more clearly in the one-eyed monk with his fair complexion and exquisitely-drawn toga with long subtle curves. Both figures have delicately drawn hands and well-placed feet, and a perfection of facial expression matched only by the mortals of the classical period. GAUTAMA, THE BUDDHA (Pl. 1), on the other hand, is a stylized Buddha with a perfect proportion of the head to the body.

The paintings in this cave are distinguished by the fact that even though the two groups of surviving pieces are separated by a period of nearly six hundred years, both groups were created at periods of stylistic transition. While the pre-Christian era painting was changing from the archaic to the classical style, the fifth century paintings such as GAUTAMA, THE BUDDHA and THE BUDDHA AND THE ONE-EYED MONK were created in the course of transition from the classical to the so-called Baroque.

Deccan in the third century, after the disappearance of the Andhra rule and the establishment of the Vakatakas. The Raja in this painting has a band of jewellery round his top-knot of hair, which is arranged like the hood of a serpent. This was emblematic, either of his mythical descent from a serpent-king or of his representing a fabulous being such as a water-spirit in human form.

On the other side of the Bodhi tree is a group of women musicians and dancers. Bare to the waist, these women do not seem to be Buddhist nuns (nuns were allowed to join the Buddhist *sangharamas* during the Buddha's own lifetime), but appear to be a party of common folk who have improvised an orchestra of their own to please the Raja and also to pay homage to the Bodhi tree. Two of the party have long trumpets and the rest are clapping their hands or dancing. The elegance of these figures conveys an atmosphere of carefree, uninhibited joy which was peculiar to this period. With its soft hues of a few colours—red ochre, yellow ochre, *terra verde*, lamp black and lime white—the painting reminds one of early Andhra art of the first century B.C. This is confirmed by the costumes, and the veils over the women's heads which are typical of early Sanchi sculptures. The features are the non-Aryan round faces and the dark skins of the people of the North-Western Deccan, which includes Ajanta. The figures in early sculptures and paintings of the Deccan possibly represent a hybrid race, a cross between the Scythians and the early inhabitants of the Deccan. From the large numbers of Megalithic tombs constructed by the Scythians, it appears that they settled down in the Deccan in the second millennium B.C. or

CAVE SIXTEEN

This *vihara*, whose plan is incised in an inscription on the left-hand wall near the end of the façade, shows the vigour and elegance of fifth century Buddhist architecture. The spacious veranda, 19.5 meters long and 3.1 meters wide, is flanked in front by six octagonal pillars and two pilasters. The hall, which is about 22 meters square and 4.6 meters high, has three entrances. The pilasters on both sides of the main doorway have sculptures of beautiful women standing on *makaras*. The hall contains twenty columns. The shrine, with a colossal Buddha, is scooped out from the back gallery of the hall, which has two side chambers. The *vihara* has no antechamber.

The principal paintings in the cave are : Scenes from the Life of the Buddha, on the rear wall of the veranda near its left end; *Sutasoma Jataka* or the story of a lioness who fell in love with Saudasa, King of Benares, on the architrave, above the front pillars of the veranda; The Demons in front of a Monastery, in the front corridor above the small door to the left of the main entrance; *Hasti Jataka* or the story of the benevolent elephant, in the front corridor to the left of the small door near the left of the main entrance; *Maha-Umagga Jataka* or the murder of a child and other episodes, on the left wall of the front corridor; The Conversion of Nanda, in the left corridor, above the doors of the first and second cells from the left; Manushi Buddhas, above the door of the third cell in the left-hand corridor; Apsarasas and the Buddha in the Teaching Attitude, on the right of the door of the fourth cell in the left-hand corridor; The Buddha in the Teaching Attitude, on the rear wall to the left of the shrine; The Elephant Procession, on the rear of the inner corridor between the shrine and the door of the second cell from the left; The Buddha preaching to the Congregation, in the rear corridor to the right of the shrine; Scenes from the Life of the Buddha, on the wall of the right-hand corridor; The First Meditation and the Four Signs, on the wall of the left-hand corridor; A Palace Scene, in the right-hand corridor above the doors of the first and second cells from the right; Scenes from the Early Life of the Buddha, between the doors of the first and second cells in the right-hand corridor.

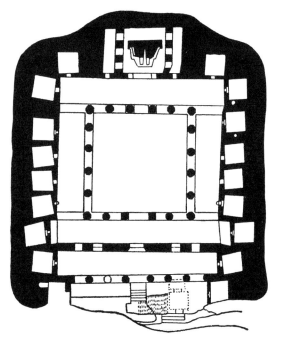

Figure 21   Plan of *Cave XVI*

NOTES ON THE PLATES

The Supernatural Child Mahosadha (Pl. 50) is a detail from the frieze depicting the *Maha-Umagga Jataka* which is painted on the left wall of the front corridor, and is continued on the adjoining pilaster. The painting was deservedly praised by Griffiths in 1874, but he was unable to copy it because the surface of the wall was at that time covered with grit and mud. It was partially cleaned by the two Italian restorers in 1920-1921. However, the gelatine they used to brighten the images soon turned yellow and opaque. This layer of gelatine has recently been removed by the Archaeological Department of the Government of India, and the detail shown here is reproduced in colour for the first time. Its subject has recently been identified by Moreshwar G. Dikshit.

The lake, garden and building shown in the painting are apparently the tank, grove and palace built by the super-natural child, which are mentioned in the Jataka. A mere seven-year-old, the boy successfully solved the riddles which were posed to him by the people to test his supernatural powers. The top left-hand corner of the painting shows a rider, representing the councillor of King Vedeha, who was deputed by his master to test Mahosadha's wisdom. He wears a coat with full sleeves and striped stockings, while a straight sword hangs by his side. One of the horse's hind legs is stretched backward and the other raised forward to convey the feeling of rapid movement. From the rider's uniform it is evident that the artists were well acquainted with the Greeks (*yavanas*), Scythians (*sakas*), and Parthians (*pahlavas*), who ruled in various parts of India for several centuries; similar costumes and accoutrements are frequently depicted in the other caves. In a plantain-grove below the royal rider there are four figures apparently representing either his servants or, more probably, the four envious councillors who attempted to destroy Mahosadha. The two men nearest to the boy have long hair, while the third wears a Persian cap. The expression of the fourth is specially sinister; his hair is dishevelled and his hand is on his sword as he looks at the boy in a wild and threatening way. The boy, wearing a small cap on his head, is gesturing to emphasize a point. The panel reproduced here is especially interesting because an illusion of distances is conveyed by depicting the group of men against a comparatively spacious background which is fringed by the conventional bands of hills. The mountains are in perfect harmony with the equally stylized water, which is represented by semi-circular arches. The barrel-shaped roofs and heavy curvilinear eaves bear a striking resemblance to the rock-hewn caves of the early fifth century. Below this scene the wall is much damaged, but a man and a woman can still be seen holding out the child's body while a soldier raises his sword to cut the boy in two. Another person with dishevelled hair looks on, but miraculously the child's execution is stopped, as the boy is again seen talking to two other people.

The famous painting, THE RENUNCIATION OF NANDA (Pl. 53), of which THE ANXIOUS MAIDENS (Pl. 52) is a detail, belongs to the great classical period. This detail, reproduced in colour for the first time, is executed in a very simple style. The traditional dignified restraint in the drawing of the sacred images is beautifully revealed. The precise expression of emotion and eloquent hand gestures of Nanda's deserted wife forcefully convey the pangs of grief at the moment of rejection. As Griffiths, who spent thirty years at Ajanta, remarked: "For pathos and sentiment and the unmistakable way of telling its story this picture, I consider, cannot be surpassed in the history of art. The Florentine could have put better drawing, and the Venetian better colour, but neither could have thrown greater expression into it." The dying woman, with drooping head, half-closed eyes and languid limbs, reclining on a bed, has none of the "prettiness" of the post-classical period.

Nanda's consort is being aided by a number of maid-servants, two of whom are seen at the left-hand end of the painting and three towards the right. The detail here shows two maids who are standing under a banana tree in an open court. As their expressions reveal, they are concerned about the dying princess. One of them has a fair skin while the other is dark. The harmony of the composition is enhanced by the pitcher with an inverted cap held by the fair maid and the sash round the neck of the other as they stand against the background of the banana tree.

On the same wall in the left corridor, above the doors of the first and second cells from the left, are painted four episodes depicting the Conversion of Nanda. The detail A MONK WATCHING THE CONVERSION OF NANDA (Pl. 74)

is here reproduced in colour for the first time. This is one of the two monks with youngish features who are watching Nanda's ordination. The style is simple and the classical flow of line has succeeded wonderfully in re-creating the serene atmosphere of the monastery. The enchantment is increased by the well-integrated composition of plain surfaces of pure soft colours, conveying a feeling of tranquillity and peace.

One of the most enchanting details from this cave, here reproduced in colour for the first time, is THE RENUNCIATION OF NANDA (Pl. 51). The young hermit sitting under a tree is the Future Buddha of the legend, who fell into a trance when his parents took him to the fields to watch the celebrations of the Sowing Festival. According to the *Jataka*, "The Sowing Festival was celebrated with great pomp. The whole city was trimmed with bunting, and the people put on new dresses and assembled at the King's palace, which, with its decorations, looked like the abode of gods. King Suddhodana took the young prince, Shadhanta, along with him to the fields to celebrate the festival. The King set out with a large retinue, and on this occasion there were one hundred and eight ploughs. The trappings of the oxen and the cross-bars of the ploughs were all ornamented with silver except for the royal plough which was ornamented with gold, as were also the horns, the reins and the goads for the oxen. In the field where the festival was to be celebrated there was a rose-apple tree (*jambu*) under which the King left his son and left attendants to watch over him. He and his attendants then began to plough. He himself drove the gold plough, his courtiers the silver ones. They tilled the soil, moving backwards and forwards with great speed until the function reached its climax. The attendants who had been left by the King to look after the Future Buddha went off to enjoy the festival. The young prince looked around him and, finding himself alone, sat down cross-legged and, mastering his breathing, entered on the first trance (First Meditation). The attendants spent their time eating, and when they returned they noticed that the shadows of the other trees had passed over towards the east while that of the rose-apple tree under which the Future Buddha was sitting, had remained stationary, encircling him like a canopy. They announced this miracle to the King, who hastened to the place and bowed before his son, saying, 'This, dear child, is my second obeisance.'"

This is one of those rare works of art in which an atmosphere of profound piety and tranquillity is produced by the simple flexing of the limbs or a gentle bending of the body, as in some of the frescoes of the Italian painters Giotto and Fra Angelico. The dignified inclination of the nurse offering food to the Future Buddha and his absent-minded response have marvellously succeeded in creating a spiritual harmony, a strong sense of vitality and an extremely effective pictorial composition.

CAVE SEVENTEEN

This *vihara*, perhaps excavated a quarter of a century after CAVE XVI, has a similar plan. The veranda, 19.5 meters long and 3 meters wide, has massive pillars in front. The main hall has three entrances, and the central door is adorned with carvings. The twenty columns dividing the corridors on the four sides of the hall, which is 19.5 meters square, are also lavishly carved and painted. The shrine, 5.5 meters by 6 meters, has an antechamber which is about 5.6 meters square. The shrine contains a massive figure of the Buddha in the *dharmacakra mudra* or Teaching attitude. The central figure is flanked by the Bodhisattva Padmapani on the right and Vajrapani on the left.

The paintings in the *vihara* are in a comparatively good condition. The most important are : A RAJA DISTRIBUTING ALMS, on the back wall of the veranda near its left end; A PALACE SCENE, on the back wall of the veranda above the window; INDRA AND APSARASAS, on the rear wall of the veranda to the left of the door; THE MANUSHI BUDDHAS AND PAIRS OF YAKSHAS AND YAKSHINIS, above the doorway in two rows; APSARASAS AND GANDHARVAS ADORING THE BUDDHA, on the rear wall of the veranda to the right of the door; THE STORY OF THE FURIOUS ELEPHANT NALAGIRI, above the two windows to the right of the main door in the rear wall of the veranda; THE BODHISATTVA AVALOKITESVARA AND THE BUDDHIST LITANY, on the outer wall of the veranda; A YAKSHA WITH A FEMALE ATTENDANT, on the left-hand wall of the veranda; THE ROYAL HUNT SCENE, on the left-hand wall of the veranda, to the left of the cell door; THE WHEEL OF SAMSARA, on the left-hand wall of the veranda above the cell door; MOTHER AND CHILD BEFORE THE BUDDHA and other Buddhist deities, on the side walls of the second window, to the right of the main entrance to the veranda; THE BUDDHA PREACHING TO THE CONGREGATION, on the right-hand wall of the veranda, above the cell door; FLORAL DESIGNS and Other Decorative Motifs, on the ceiling of the veranda; *Shaddanta Jataka*, or the story of the six-tusked elephant, on the outer wall of the front corridor, left of the main entrance; *Mahakapi Jataka*, on the wall of the front corridor to the left of the main entrance; *Hasti Jataka*, or the story of the benevolent elephant, on the wall of the front corridor, to the left of the main entrance; THE BESTOWAL OF THE ROYAL SWORD, on the left-hand wall of the front corridor; A COURT SCENE, on the left-hand wall of the front corridor, above the cell door; *Hamsa Jataka* or the story of the golden goose, on the left wall and the adjoining pilaster of the front corridor, to the right of the cell door; SARDULAS, APSARASAS AND THE BUDDHA IN THE TEACHING ATTITUDE, on the pilaster between the front and the left corridors; *Visvantara Jataka*, or the story of the Prince devoted to alms-giving, on the wall of the left-hand corridor; FIGURES OF A YAKSHA AND YAKSHINI AND APSARASAS, on the pilaster between the left and back corridors; *Mahakapi Jataka*, or the story of the benevolent monkey, on the left-hand wall of the back corridor; *Sutasoma Jataka*, or the story of the pious King of Indraprastha trying to persuade Saudasa, the King of Benares, to give up cannibalism, on the wall of the rear corridor to the left of the antechamber; THE BUDDHA PREACHING IN THE TUSHITA HEAVEN, on the left-hand wall of the antechamber; MOTHER AND CHILD BEFORE THE BUDDHA, on the rear wall of the antechamber, to the left of the shrine door; THE GREAT MIRACLE OF SRAVASTI, on the right-hand wall of the antechamber; *Sarabha Jataka*, or the story of the merciful stag, on the rear wall of the back corridor, right of the antechamber; *Matriposhaka Jataka*, or the story of the elephant who had blind parents, on the rear wall of the back corridor between the first and second doors to the right of the antechamber; *Matsya Jataka*, or the story of the fish which saved its kin from certain death, on the rear wall of the back corridor, right of the antechamber; *Syama Jataka*, or the story of a young hermit whose parents were blind, on the rear wall of the back corridor; *Mahisha Jataka*, or the story of the benevolent buffalo and the mischievous monkey, on the right-hand wall of the rear corridor, to the left of the cell door; A YAKSHA OR A ROYAL GUARD, on the face of the pilaster between the right and rear corridors; *Simhala Avadana*, covering the entire wall of the right-hand corridor and continued on the upper part of the pilaster between this corridor and the one behind it; A LADY IN THE BEAUTY PARLOUR, on the upper part of the pilaster between the front and right corridors; *Sibi Jataka* or the story of the king who gave his eyes away, on the pilaster between the front and right corridors and continued on the right-hand

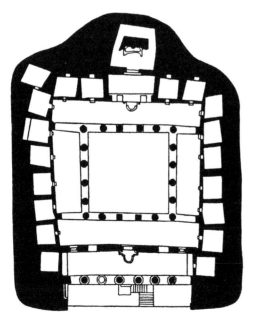

Figure 22   Plan of *Cave XVII*

wall of the front corridor; *Mriga Jataka*, or the story of the golden deer, on the wall of the front corridor; THE STORY OF THE BENEVOLENT BEAR, on the wall of the front corridor; *Nigrodhamiga Jataka*, or the story of the sacred deer who offered his life in place of that of a doe, on the wall of the

front corridor; TWO DWARFS WITH MUSICAL INSTRUMENTS, on the base of a pillar in the antechamber; FLORAL DESIGNS and Other Motifs, on the ceilings of the hall and the corridors; THE BUDDHA PREACHING TO THE CONGREGATION, painted over the door of the third cell in the left-hand aisle.

NOTES ON THE PLATES

Although the sixty-one distinct scenes which Burgess described in his notes many years ago no longer exist, this cave still contains the largest number of painted pieces. Alms-giving being the first of the Ten Perfections of the Buddhist faith, this subject is frequently seen at Ajanta, but no other is as spectacular as A RAJA DISTRIBUTING ALMS (Pl. 60) which is painted on the back wall of the veranda towards the left end. Some have identified the story with the anecdote in the *Vishvantara Jataka*, in which the prince, when he was four or five years old, gave away his most valuable necklace to his nurse. When the King was informed

Plate 82   A detail from the ceiling of *Cave XVII*

of the gift he replaced it with an equally valuable necklace worth one hundred thousand pieces of gold. Vishvantara, however, gave away this necklace too, and repeated the gift nine times. In this panoramic scene showing a large crowd of ascetics and mendicants, to whom food and other gifts are being given, the King is seen sitting with his consort on a throne which is placed near an areca-nut tree, while a young girl and a child are bringing trays of offerings

to the royal couple. The monarch is as usual surrounded by guards in colourful uniforms, trying to control a large crowd of ascetics and others who are attempting to force their way forward in order to pay homage. To the right are two horses, supposed to be the animals which Vishvantara gave as gifts to the four Brahmins. Above the crowd there is a canopy bearing five monks or holy men. This is a landmark in style, in which the classical phase, having quickly reached its zenith, begins to show the first signs of Mannerism. In this phase of artistic development the figures are sophisticated, refined yet sympathetic, their expressions are animated and their costumes elaborate, while the composition as a whole is harmonious. The *Simhala Avadana* painting is one of the best examples of this period.

On the back wall of the veranda towards the right of the door is the lyrical representation of APSARASAS AND GANDHARVAS ADORING THE BUDDHA (Pl. 69). The mystic ecstasy of Kalidasa's poetry, the inspiration for which was derived from religious and moral sources, is depicted in this frieze with an incredible effect. The floating clouds, the swaying foliage and the heavenly bodies, *apsarasas* and *gandharvas* flying swiftly through the air, produce a fantastic sense of movement and excitement. The artist was perhaps aware of the passage in the *Vishnudharmottara* which states : "He who paints waves, flames, smoke, streamers fluttering in the air, according to the movement of the wind, should be considered a great painter." The finest of the figures in this panel is an *apsaras* or heavenly nymph whose rapid flight through the air is indicated by her swaying necklace of sapphires and pearls and the ribbons and scarves which are shown fluttering behind her. She holds cymbals and wears a turban with astonishing decorative detail. A RAJA DISTRIBUTING ALMS, on the other side of the door, is painted in the same style.

Above the main entrance leading to the main hall of this cave there is a row of eight figures, the seven Manushi Buddhas and Maitreya, which in style are very similar to GAUTAMA, THE BUDDHA (Pl. 1). According to the Buddhist legend, Maitreya will succeed Gautama. One notable feature in these panels is that they all contain foliage of various trees in the background. Some of these have been destroyed but one can still notice banian leaves over the head in the sixth, the pipal over the head in the seventh and the ashoka over the head in the eighth. Below this row, on the lintel, are eight panels of *mithuna* figures, either sipping wine, caressing each other or talking in an amorous manner. The varied tones of their skins, as shown in A YAKSHA AND HIS CONSORT (Pls. 55 and 56), display a remarkable sense of colour and a controlled rhythm in the draftsmanship. The technique is similar to that which inspired the fine design and balanced composition of the two friezes. A RAJA DISTRIBUTING ALMS, APSARASAS AND GANDHARVAS ADORING THE BUDDHA, and all these paintings in the veranda make a delightful introduction to this magnificent cave.

The entire ceiling of the veranda, in conformity with the tradition, is divided into panels depicting creepers and floral designs of great variety. The flowers are painted at different stages of their unfolding, and ornamental stems, waterfowl and diminutive human figures all add to the delightful pattern. Colour such as green, yellow, white, and black have been freely employed but blue is rare.

THE BABY ELEPHANT (Pl. 5) and THE MONKEY BENEATH A PALAS TREE (Pl. 3) are details, reproduced here in colour for the first time, from the frieze SHADDANTA IN A LOTUS LAKE (Pl. 66). The painter has drawn Shaddanta just as he is described in the *Jataka*. The mass of the Bodhisattva stands out from the life around him, yet still remains a part of the warm and lively scene. This is the world's largest drawing of this period of an elephant. The story is depicted in four episodes : first, the bedroom scene in which the Rani plans her revenge; second, the lotus lake in which Shaddanta is bathing and sporting with his herd; third, the hunters bringing the tusks of the Bodhisattva to the royal court; and in the fourth scene the Rani faints on seeing them. SHADDANTA IN A LOTUS LAKE depicts the second episode in which the six-tusked elephant is sporting with his herd in the beautiful lake. The charming lotus flowers on the surface of the water, the elephant-herd plucking flowers as offerings for their lord, the belt of hills where the animals, wolves and apes, and tribesmen are surrounded by ferns and creepers with leaves of exquisite shape, all vividly suggest the animals' care-free life in the jungle. Another very sympathetic drawing of elephants in this cave is THE FREED ELEPHANT MEETS HIS BLIND MOTHER (Pl. 76). It is a painting which owes its quality not so much to acute observation as to a deep sense of kinship with nature. The story depicted here is slightly different from that given in the *Jataka* but it agrees with the version recorded in the Chinese text (translated by E. Chavannes) which states that the Bodhisattva's parents were both blind and he treated them with great affection. The story is painted here in two parts, one above the other. In the upper part the royal court is depicted, where the forester gave the information leading to the elephant's capture. On the right the elephant is shown as he is being brought to the court stable. In the lower part of the painting two more episodes are represented, showing the recapture of the sacred elephant and his return to his blind parents after his release.

As the elephant, the horse and the deer stood respectively for the Conception, the Great Renunciation and the First Sermon, a dignified restraint is seen in the drawing of these animals. A HORSE (Pl. 73) is a beautiful example. The majestic poise of the neck and head, like the Bankura terracottas from Bengal, surpasses the portrayal of many of the monarchs of Ajanta. The importance of drawing horses is evident from a whole chapter on this subject in the ancient Indian treatise, the *Sukranitisara*, by Sukracarya. The detail reproduced here is from the first of the two episodes from the *Mahakapi Jataka*. This episode depicts the arrival of the Raja of Benares on the banks of the river Ganges, where he orders his archers to shoot the monkey. In the second episode, from which THE RAJA AND HIS GROOM LISTENING TO THE SACRED MONKEY (Pl. 59) is a detail, the Bodhisattva is teaching the doctrine of the Buddha. The insertion of the horse's head in between the figure of the Raja and his groom is an indication of the absence of any dividing line between the human beings and animals.

The two enchanting details, A PAIR OF ANTELOPES (Pl. 18) and A FOREST SCENE (Pl. 19), even though considerably effaced, show the essential forms of the drawing and the delicacy achieved with bold vigorous lines. There is not much detail left, but the sweeping lines are so freely drawn that one scarcely regrets the effacement which has laid bare such vital and basic structures. While in the portrayal of human and divine figures there are fluctuations and changes in style, it is worth noting that in the depiction of animals and birds the artists have maintained considerable consistency and continuity. These details, which are reproduced in colour for the first time, are from the *Mriga Jataka*. While the elephants, horses and deer are drawn with great precision of line and confidence of draftsmanship, the artists have singularly failed in drawing dogs, as can be seen in A MAN WITH A DOG (Pl. 57) from the *Mriga Jataka*. It seems as if the failure were due to its not being a traditional subject; nor was the dog popular as a Bodhisattva.

The mastery in portraying animals is also seen in THE FOWLER AND THE GOLDEN GEESE (Pl. 65). The *Mahahamsa Jataka*, from which this detail is taken, must have been very popular at Ajanta because it is also depicted in CAVE II. In this *vihara* the story is painted in two episodes. In the first part the hunters are seen catching the sacred bird and his chief adviser in the lotus lake. The second part depicts a court scene in which the sacred goose is teaching the Law of the Buddha to the Raja of Benares and his consort. In terms of style these birds are identical with THE DOVE (Pl. 4) in CAVE II; although the firm brush strokes have given the birds an appearance of solidity and firmness, the composition and their movements in the air are most natural. The position of this painting on the left wall and the adjoining pilaster of the front corridor, to the right of the cell door, is well chosen because it has intensified the image of a trap from which the birds are frantically struggling to escape.

This magnificent large panel with its bold and ambitious composition, painted over the entire wall of the right corridor, depicts the *Simhala Avadana*. It is a monumental frieze so eloquent in expression, so vivacious and varied in design and so full of beautiful forms and colours that it is undoubtedly one of the most outstanding contributions to the classical art of Ajanta. It depicts tales of adventure, shipwrecks, seduction by beautiful women, elopements, wars and conquests, which as a composite whole are unparalleled in the history of Indian painting. The colourful horses, decorated elephants, and expressive faces are executed with unsurpassed skill. Also in keeping with the classical style is the fact that the ladies wear few ornaments and their coiffures are modest. The story begins with the ship-wreck scene, which is painted a little above ground-level between the third and fourth cell door. It proceeds towards the top of the fourth cell door, then turns to the left, spreads to the end of the wall, and also covers the upper part of the pilaster. Then it again turns downwards, occupying the wall between the first and the third cell doors. The portion of the painting showing the ship-wreck is much damaged but the other scenes depicting the landing of the merchants, their dallying with the ogresses and their ultimate victory can still be seen fairly clearly.

THE OGRESSES (Pl. 75) is one of the most outstanding studies in expression at Ajanta. The grotesque figures are about to devour all the merchants whom they have enticed to their island, while A MERCHANT IN THE ISLAND OF OGRESSES (Pl. 9) is waiting for a chance to escape. The line work of the fresco is largely obliterated but some of the details such as MONKS IN A MONASTERY (Pl. 12) show refined taste in the choice of expression and poses and consummate skill in the blending of colours. The arrangement of the figures here displays a wonderful sense of perspective, and the painting is infused with a feeling of animation by the way in which the monks are talking among themselves. The artist's perfect command of drawing could not be better demonstrated than by this painting where, even though the colours have largely vanished the basic structure and essential form are still revealed. The original tones and the brilliance of the colours are shown in a piece of freshly-cleaned plaster (Pl. 13). A MONASTERY (Pl. 30) is a notable example showing the artist's proficiency in structural perspective. The planimetric construction of a skeletal framework made up of alternately shaded bands of lintels and posts receding into space creates a perfect illusion of a third dimension. The Monastery at once seems to establish a concord with the architectural atmosphere of the cave, a cubism produced by the vertical and horizontal flat surfaces of the walls in relation to the empty spaces.

Similar keen observation of the vertico-horizontal relationship of the cave interiors is used in depicting the street scenes, such as THE ROYAL KITCHEN OF KING SAUDASA (Pl. 49). Here a strange pictorial magic, conjured up by geometrical virtuosity, is balanced by the "reality" of the figure drawings. The scene is a detail from the *Sutasoma Jataka*, and was identified for the first time by Foucher in 1920. The story begins with a lioness enamoured by the beauty of a prince whom she had found sleeping under a tree, and becoming pregnant by licking the soles of his feet. The offspring of this strange love, named Saudasa, was reared and trained as a prince, but eventually developed a passion for human flesh. The several episodes of the story are painted on the wall of the back corridor with a great deal of imagination and skill. They show the King of Benares setting out on a hunt with his retinue, accompanied by two other princes and a pack of dogs. The King is then seen pursuing the deer and, having become separated from his retinue, entering a forest abounding in wild animals. The nimble movement of the deer and the wild stare in its eyes are shown in THE DEER HUNT (Pl. 77). In this unsurpassed masterpiece, the horror of being hunted and killed is marvellously conveyed by the animal's abrupt and swift leap and the almost hypnotised look in its bulging eyes as it glances

back at the approaching horse. The forest scene continues above this panel and the King, exhausted by his efforts, is shown asleep under a tree. The lioness approaches the King, and licks the soles of his feet. A similar scene then shows the lioness proceeding to the King's palace after passing through the bazaar. Apparently special preparations had been made to receive the lioness, for the path is strewn with flowers and there is a line of flags on one side of the road, which is crowded with spectators. On the other side there is a row of shops, and half-clad tribesmen with unkempt hair, and with flat circular vessels in front of and around them. The next scene represents the royal court, where the King is sitting on the throne with a child in his lap while the lioness stands before him. He is surrounded by courtiers. The scene to the left of this probably represents an *abhisheka* ceremony, which is performed at the time of a prince's enthronement. THE ROYAL KITCHEN OF KING SAUDASA is close by. The cook is apparently preparing human flesh, since a man is shown impaled with a spear which has passed through his chest and back. This is the sole example of sadistic realism in Ajanta art. But at the same time, to emphasize the people's aversion to cannibalism, the painter has shown two more scenes, which are followed by another scene showing King Saudasa sitting in a state of perplexity in his royal pavilion because he realized the Sin. Among the courtiers is A LADY AT THE COURT OF SAUDASA (Pl. 71) which is here reproduced in colour for the first time. It is among the finest examples of the Mannerist style of drawing women. This figure strikes a balance between the absolute Hinayana concepts of simplicity and the dignified restraint which is characteristic of the classical style. Lastly, on the left wall of the back corridor, the army which has come to protect Sutasoma is shown. The subject appears to be a scene from the battle which followed the capture of Sutasoma by Saudasa. The archers stretching their bowstrings, the warriors brandishing their swords, the heavy thud of the elephants and trotting of the horses are a wonderful climax to this *Jataka*. In style this painting is similar to AN ARMY ON THE MARCH (Pl. 72), which perhaps also represents an episode from the *Sutasoma Jataka*.

Another beautiful frieze on the left wall of this cave depicts the *Vishvantara Jataka*. Since reproductions of subjects from this panel are easily accessible, only two more unusual pieces are shown here, reproduced in colour for the first time. These are THE COURTIER (Pl. 22) and ONE OF THE RAJA'S ATTENDANTS (Pl. 58). The sensuous exuberance of the saturated splashes of brilliant red in both these paintings is especially striking in THE COURTIER, with its effective side-light in the manner of Rembrandt or Caravaggio, produced by specks of yellow infusing luminosity and giving a three dimensional quality.

Except for THE LADY AT HER TOILET (Pl. 63), which is well-known, all the portraits of women in this book, such as A LADY OF THE COURT (Pl. 61), A WOMAN IN A COURT SCENE (Pl. 64), SUJATA, THE FARMER'S DAUGHTER (Pl. 70) and other plates already described, are reproduced in colour for the first time. THE LADY AT HER TOILET which belongs to the late period, is repeated mainly for the contrast it provides with the so-called Mannerist style of the other pictures of women reproduced in this volume.

LIST OF PLATES

LIST OF FIGURES

BIBLIOGRAPHY

G. Yazdani and others, Ajanta, Parts I-IV, Oxford 1930-1955.

S. Kramrisch, A Survey of Painting in the Deccan, London 1937.

B. Rowland, The Wall Paintings of India, Central asia and Ceylon, Boston 1938.

S. Paramasivan, Indian Wall Paintings, Journal of Madras University vols. XII 1940
and XIII 1941.

Philip S. Rawson, Indian Painting, New York 1961.

C. L. Fabri, Frescoes of Ajanta : an Essay, Marg Vol. IX n° 1, 1956.

H. Goetz, Painting: Ajanta, Marg Vol. IX n° 2, 1956.

S. Kramrisch, Vishnudharmottara, Calcutta 1928.

Douglas Barrett, Painting of India, Geneva 1963.

Madanjeet Singh, India, Paintings from Ajanta Caves, Paris 1954.

Ananda K. Coomaraswamv, The Transformation of Nature in Art,
New York 1934.

I. B. Horner, Translation of Vinaya Pitaka, London 1949.

S. Radhakrishnan, Gautama, the Buddha, Bombay 1938.

E. B. Cowell, Jataka Stories, London 1957.

Karl Khandalavala, Indian Sculpture and Painting, Bombay 1938.

G. Yazdani, The Early History of the Deccan, Parts I-VI, Oxford 1960.

Mulk Raj Anand, Aurangabad Caves, Marg Vol. XVI n° 3, 1963.

Alan Moorehead, Lovers Upon the Walls, The New Yorker May,1, 1954.

This book was produced by Société d'Editions EDITA, Lausanne
and printed in offset by Imprimerie Paul Attinger SA, Neuchâtel
The edition was bound by Mayer & Soutter SA, Lausanne

June 1965